Liberation IS

The End Of The Spiritual Path

Salvadore Poe

Published by Liberation IS Publishing

Liberation IS: The End of the Spiritual Path

www.liberationis.com
www.salvadorepoe.com

Paperback:
ISBN - 13: 978-1-7321411-3-1
ISBN - 10: 1-7321411-3-4

eBook:
ISBN - 13: 978-1-7321411-2-4
ISBN - 10: 1-7321411-2-6

Transcribed by: Lola Lozano and Donna Holt
Edited by: Ron Gorayeb, Lola Lozano and Al Kuehn
Proofread by: Seth Colby, Ryan Cramer and Robert Middleton
Cover Design: Elena Skaya and Salvadore Poe
Photo of Salvadore: Elena Skaya, www.elenaskaya.com

Table of Contents

PREFACE

In the course of preparing this book, it became evident that I should speak a bit about what brought me to do this work. Until the age of thirty-nine, I had no interest at all in matters of enlightenment, liberation, spirituality or whatever you may call it. When I was a late teenager, having been in Catholic high school and seeing nothing in the whole religious environment that appealed or spoke to me, I summarily dismissed it all and never thought about it again.

For the next twenty years, I pursued a career in music, and along with that a lifestyle of partying and abusing drugs and alcohol. I was not unhappy but was just bored with ordinary consciousness and looking for a heightened experience of life. I was a seeker in the realm of the mundane—success, acclaim, money, drugs, and alcohol—and had some of all of those.

One day, in February 1997, after a night of extreme excess, I found myself looking out of my East Village, Avenue A apartment in Manhattan, feeling the noonday sun, seeing everyone outside doing their thing, and knowing without a doubt in my mind that I had destroyed my life. I was completely devastated and crushed. In a moment of total desperation, with not a shred of hope, and with all sense of security ripped away, I fell, with no volition of my own, to my knees in an anguished plea for help. This was not a plea to god or anyone else; it was just, "HELP ME!"

With the amount of drugs I had in my body at that time, there was no way on earth I would be able to sleep. But, immediately after that plea, I did indeed fall asleep. Three hours later, I woke up and knew something had remarkably changed. I knew exactly what I needed to do. I walked right away to a bookstore in Saint Mark's Place and straight to the Eastern philosophy section I had once seen. I picked three books by authors I had heard of—Thich Nhat Hahn, Osho, and J. Krishnamurti. From that moment on, drugs, alcohol and cigarettes were finished, with no effort or struggle. So began my seeking in the spiritual realm.

I began reading every book I could find and tried to meditate. Very early on in my seeking days, I had a strange experience. While sitting on a bus, I spontaneously began going back in time through my life. At each point along the way, progressing backward to when I was a very young child, I experienced my life circumstances as if I were there then, seeing out of the eyes of the person I was at that time. In each moment, no matter how far back I went, no matter how different my body and mind were from now, I saw that I had not changed even one iota. I was the same always. And then going forward in time until old age, I experienced the same thing. I thought, "How can it be that I have not changed at all even though everything about me has changed so much?" Unable to see the implication of this revelation, and certainly not yet ready to be finished by it, I chalked it off to just a peculiar experience.

In early 1998, I went to India for the first time on a spiritual retreat. During that retreat, I began having mystical experiences and states of such incredible intensity, ecstasy, sublimity, revelation, and transcendence that I was stunned. Completely and radically different states of consciousness than I had ever known, I had no idea things like this were possible. No drug experience I ever had could compare.

Over the next couple of years, I continued having these experiences and more and more I wanted to be in India. But in the meantime, I went on several meditation retreats in the USA, Sweden, and France. I also met many teachers—U.G. Krishnamurti, Douglas Harding, and Toni Packer (all of whom I still admire) as well as any other teacher that was passing through wherever I might be.

In 2002, four years after my first visit to India, I returned and went to visit a sage named Ajja in Southern India. For some reason, he took a liking to me and so I stayed mostly there for two years, meditating eight hours a day. But after two years, the concept of liberation was foremost in my mind and even after all of the spiritual experiences I had, and after living with this authentic sage, I was not satisfied. In 2004, I left Ajja and went to Tiruvannamalai, the home of Ramana Maharshi.

Again, I began meditating many hours each day. But now, after seven years of meeting teachers with no real results, I was no longer interested in meeting another. Someone told me about a silent sage named Siva Sakthi. He really stressed that I should go, but I was not interested. Eventually, he convinced me just to check her out. As soon as I saw her, I felt she was very authentic. She never spoke, she just sat there in silence, but her authenticity was evident. A week later, I moved into her small ashram, the first person other than her son (her caretaker) to live there. Over the next nine months, I meditated all the time and had many more mystical experiences and transcendent states of consciousness.

In November of 2004, having had so many experiences, I was getting frustrated. Where is this thing called liberation? Why every time one of these experiences came and I was convinced this was it, did it then pass and leave me the same? When will the final, permanent experience happen? I felt that I would need to find a very secluded place and just live out my life in meditation.

Around this time, someone passing through Tiruvannamalai told me I should go see this teacher in Pune named Dolano. On hearing her name and reading the words, "The Last Satsang" on her website, I knew I had to go. Two weeks later, I was in Pune sitting with her. On the very first day, I recognized my essential being of freedom. I knew that this was what had revealed itself to me on that bus eight years ago, but I had not yet had the eyes to recognize its implication.

This very ordinary and obvious recognition, along with the inquiries she suggested, over time, simply ended all doubts and misidentifications until there was nothing left but the knowing, "I am free." Seeking was finished; there was no cause of it any longer.

After that, with my spiritual path finished, I kept living mostly in India and went back to making music again. In 2012, eight years after my meeting with Dolano, and with no inclination to become a teacher or anything like that, someone asked me to share. I was very reluctant.

Finally, I agreed to speak with one person, with the caveat that I would only continue if what I wanted to share truly worked.

By that, I meant that someone recognizes their essential free nature and is finished seeking. I found my own way of sharing, out of a need to do it, and so this work was born. Since then, I have seen many of the people who have contacted me come to the end of their spiritual, esoteric and philosophical beliefs, recognize that they are free, and be finished with spiritual seeking. I am amazed and happy each and every time.

To this day, my only interest with each person I work with is for them to recognize their free, essential being and be finished seeking. I simply point out, through inquiries, some things that you may not have noticed before until this recognition is clear. I then spend time to make sure all questions are answered and it is doubtless.

I am not a guru or a spiritual teacher. There are not and never will be ashrams, sanghas, disciples, students, followers, etc. In my opinion, the days of all of that are over.

This book is a record of more than two years of this work, taken from many different inquiry sessions with numerous people. There are inquiries, experiments, questions and answers, and other dialogues between me and inquirers in one-on-one and group sessions. My hope for this book is the same as above—that you, the reader, come to know for yourself what is true, which is that you are now and always have been free, and to be finished seeking.

Salvadore Poe, Tiruvannamalai, India

EDITORS' FOREWORDS

Ron

When the Buddha was asked if he was enlightened, he responded, "I am awake." I had often wondered why he would respond that way. Perhaps the word "enlightened" was loaded then just as it is today. Most people have notions of what it means to be enlightened; their notions border on fantasies. Some think it means you walk around in bliss, others think it means nothing ever bothers you. Some think it bestows you with magical powers. I used to have these notions as well. Perhaps Buddha chose his response to avoid the baggage associated with the notions of enlightenment.

I met Salvadore in March of 2012. I had been a seeker for some forty years. In the early years, I sought in the material world—wealth, sex, success. That then morphed into developing mastery of techniques like creative visualization, intuitive perception, and healing techniques; that morphed into adding a dimension of spirituality and then toward seeking enlightenment. I attained quite a bit of success in the material and mental world, but enlightenment eluded me.

I was both diligent and intense in my pursuit of enlightenment. My close friend and fellow seeker had basically given up seeking enlightenment and figured he'd let me do all the seeking. He thought that with my intense pursuit if anyone would get there, I would, and then he would latch on. I met and worked with many enlightened (and allegedly enlightened) people and participated in many different intensives. My last venture was to work with a shaman and take hallucinogens to make inroads into my true nature.

Forty years, endless paths, and still no enlightenment. I believed I was ready but here I was, just regular old me.

The people who introduced me to the shaman later introduced me to a woman whom they thought could help me. She was not up to the task but did recommend I speak to an awakened man in India named Sal. She said he was authentic and that he could help me. I later learned she had to convince Sal to work with me as he was not interested in teaching or having students. He finally agreed to do so on the condition that if it didn't work he would just stop. He had never taken on a student and wasn't sure he wanted to.

I assumed Sal was an abbreviation for an Indian name, but I found out he's from New Jersey. He and I emailed, and we set up a time to talk on Skype. I was about to work one-on-one with an enlightened individual! That was three years ago. Since meeting Sal, my notions about enlightenment and my core beliefs about reality have been upended.

I have changed. Not in a big way but in subtle, nuanced ways. I still have fears and anxieties, but they no longer have me in their grip. They are more like an appearance, something temporary just showing up and passing through. I don't hold onto them, I don't even engage. They appear, linger briefly and then disappear. As a result, I am more relaxed, at ease, comfortable in the universe. And when my world is upside down, in disarray, I take it in stride like I never have before. And I have more and more moments of being so authentically present that I experience the wonder and the "is-ness" of each moment in a way I have never done before.

I am no longer one of Sal's students, which is his intention. I am no longer a seeker of enlightenment. If you ask me if I am enlightened, I will simply say, "I am finished seeking."

What we have attempted to do in this book is to take you on the journey that Sal guided me and numerous other inquirers on, so that you come to the recognition of your essential being and come to the end of seeking.

Ron Gorayeb, New Jersey, USA

Lola

Finding out who I am in essence has been the simplest, yet most powerful thing that has happened to me. After a long journey, which included many meditation retreats, yoga, working with energy, therapy, healing, purifying and many other seeking activities, I was tired and felt I was getting nowhere.

Then one day, browsing the Internet, looking for spiritual teachings as I did every single day for hours on end, I suddenly bumped into a YouTube video of someone called Salvadore Poe. There was nothing fancy about the video, but I deeply felt that what was being said was true. I visited his website and read that he did inquiry sessions over the Internet. On Skype, a few days later, I met this ordinary—yet free—man, and for some reason, I absolutely knew that he could help me. I completed the inquiry sessions, and they changed what I knew about myself, forever.

After that, there was no more looking for teachers and retreats, and no more spiritual seeking. Knowing who I am— essentially free, unborn, whole and complete—was all I needed to know. Sal, in the most direct and simple way, pointed out this essential truth from the beginning. Several more inquiry sessions and experiments and looking at what is already the case from different angles, made this knowing more and more doubtless.

I am forever grateful for his loving dedication to showing people what's true. As I later transcribed other people's sessions and worked with Sal on the making of this book, I could see how he was able to help many people in seeing their true nature directly. His only concern is for inquirers to recognize, in their own direct experience, what is already here and what, once pointed out clearly and effectively, is so simple and obvious.

After recognizing who we really are, life's problems, difficulties, and ups and downs are still there, but knowing our silent and timeless essential nature makes a big difference. Objects and events come and go in who we are, without touching this spacious essence. My eternal and deepest gratitude to Sal for guiding me and others towards noticing and getting to know this eternal truth.

Lola Lozano, Puebla, MEXICO

ENGAGING WITH THIS BOOK

This book is not intended as another spiritual book, of which there are already thousands. It is intended to help you to be finished seeking. And it is not intended as a means to transcend your humanity, but to embrace your humanity in total. For this to happen, you will need to clearly recognize what each inquiry is pointing to. If you just read it as a page-turner, anxious to get through it, it will have little impact or benefit. This work is not about understanding or gaining more spiritual information. It is about recognizing what is being pointed to, not understanding it. But if you go slowly, read carefully, follow the suggestions and do the experiments, it can help you to recognize your free essential being and come to the end of seeking.

Read the book sequentially from start to finish. If you skip around or choose your favorite sounding chapters to go to, it won't work. If you just read the first inquiry and have a recognition and think that is enough, you will be missing a lot. There is a progression to the book and it needs to be seen all the way through.

Take it step by step. If at first you think it is too simple and obvious, keep reading and doing the experiments. It leads to more relief and relaxation of beliefs and eventually doubtlessness. You will see for yourself.

You will find that certain things are repeated many times in this book. This is not meant to insult your intelligence. It is because it's easy to gloss over important points, and these points need to be seen many times for this to work. Because of the ingrained ideas and concepts we have in our mind, it can take several readings to really hear something new and have these ideas released.

This is not a self-help book, a book about morality or right behavior, or a book about how to live. The only intention is to help you recognize your free essential being and come to the end of seeking. Everything is for that purpose. It does not matter at all what I or any teacher or guru knows. It only matters what you know for yourself. So be sure that you see for yourself if what is pointed to is true or not. If it is true, you will then know for yourself. Don't believe anything you read, see for yourself if it is true.

The paragraphs are arranged with a space between each. This is to slow you down a beat, so that what you just read will sink in a bit more. It is hoped that by the end of these Inquiries you will never need another spiritual teacher or teaching again. There is an end to all of that.

INTRODUCTION TO THE INQUIRIES

WHAT IS LIBERATION AND ENLIGHTENMENT?

When we are seekers on the spiritual path we gain many ideas about enlightenment and liberation from reading books and listening to teachers. In my own experience—which was eight years of intensive meditation, reading countless books, traveling around the world meeting and even living with teachers, and having many mystical experiences—I had many ideas of what this thing called liberation was going to be when it happened. Every one of them was wrong.

The main idea that almost everyone has is that enlightenment or liberation has something to do with an experience. We are going to have an experience that is going to elevate us into a new transcendent state of consciousness. When I was seeking, I had experiences like that, and whether they lasted a minute, an hour, a week or a month, they all came and they all went. And I was always left right back where I was before, wondering what happened to the experience, what happened to enlightenment and why I was still the same.

The thing about experiences (good ones, bad ones, pleasant and unpleasant, mundane and transcendental) is that they are all equal. By that I mean that they all come and they all go. They are all appearances. Experience by its very nature is not intended to last forever. It is an object in consciousness that appears and then disappears. There is no experience that is going to come and last for the rest of your life.

What we come to believe, and I believed it too, is that in all of these incredible mystical experiences, the experience is "it." The experience is enlightenment, and if it lasts forever, I will be enlightened. What we fail to see is that I am aware of the experience. No matter what the experience is, I am aware of it. So, what we need to find out is who is this that is aware, because that is what doesn't come and go. What we come to know in these inquiries is what doesn't change. What never changes and is always the same. In coming to know that, it becomes possible for this mind to be liberated from seeking.

THE CAROUSEL OF MIND — THREE MODELS FOR SEEKING HEALTH

Liberation is true mental and emotional health and stability. There are three models we have explored our whole lives to come to this health. The first one is the psychological (i.e. Freudian) model. We look inside the mind, dig into the past, explore our experiences, analyze why they happened, and why they are causing us to be the way we are now. This is the carousel of mind. We get on this carousel of mind and go around in circles forever, it's endless. We are trying to straighten out the ego, correct it, fix it, get rid of it, reorganize, and understand it. But when you are on the carousel of mind, you just go around in circles. And by believing there is truth in there, you reify the belief in ego/self.

Some of us move past that model and get on the philosophical carousel of mind. Now, I am going to understand the meaning of life. I read Aristotle, Nietzsche or whomever else. I am going to understand: why am I here? where did I come from? how shall I live? and what is the meaning of life? All of these philosophies are again the carousel of mind/self. So, we end up doing the same thing, reifying self, and we never get off the carousel.

When some of us realize that the mental and philosophical models don't work, we get on the spiritual carousel of mind. Mystical experiences, uniting with the divine, spiritual understanding, esoteric practices, devotion to God, talking to transcendent masters, and so on. Whatever our spiritual thing might be, it is all mind and we never get off that carousel. Mind, in this example, is self, ego. So, we never get off these three carousels, we just keep going around in circles supporting the belief in a separate self.

JUMP

We can see that through these three different models we never come to something essential. We just support the belief in a separate self who is trying to solve all of its problems by following these different mental strategies. It is basically self-improvement. True mental and emotional stability is not attained by continually trying to modify our thoughts. So then, what do we do?

We jump off all of it. Just jump. That is the only way. Beliefs, concepts, ideas and experiences are what make up this so-called self. It is all in the mind, and if you want to see beyond self and find liberation, you need to jump. To discover the natural, free, already liberated condition, we need to stop searching in the thought structure.

Psychology is valuable for many people who are mentally unbalanced and need to come to some semblance of mental health. So, I support psychology for that purpose. Philosophy, while maybe an interesting mental exercise, has no value at all for liberation. Spirituality is just an illusion. It can be fun and entertaining, and make you feel good sometimes. It can give a sense of hope and some semblance of security, if that is all one wants. But, as far as liberation, it is useless. It has no relation to liberation at all.

YOUR BIRTH

When were you born? What date, time and year did you come out of the womb? This is when we are told we were born. But is that true? Let's find out.

Birth means coming to life, right? From no life, coming to life. But, before you came out of the womb at a particular time and place, while you were inside the womb, life was present, wasn't it? Before the embryo there was a sperm and an egg. Life was present in each. It's not sperm life and egg life, it's just life. Like an electrical socket in the wall, one wire goes to your TV and the other to your radio. But how many electricities are there? One. Sperm, egg, life. Just life. Before the sperm and egg, life was present in your parents' bodies. And before them, life was present in your grandparents, etc. Before humans, life was present in the dinosaurs, reptiles, fish, and single cell amoebas. Life has always been present.

Then, in your parents' bodies, a sperm and an egg are created and they come together. But is life created? No, only a new form is created. Then that splits into different cells—form is changing. But life has been present since the amoeba, all the way to now, the present. Form keeps changing, into an embryo, then a fetus, then it comes out of the body and they say you were born. So then, what was born?

If you weren't born then, when were you born? Or were you born? There is a story in the Bible that speaks about this. There was this guy named Adam. He was in the Garden of Eden. Eden is perfect, pure. Adam lacks nothing and is complete and whole. God says to Adam, "Do whatever you like. Enjoy. Just don't do one thing. Don't eat the fruit from that tree, the tree of knowledge." The knowledge is of good and evil, which just means duality. But one day, Adam gets tempted and takes a bite from that fruit. So, if he takes a bite of the fruit from the tree of knowledge, then he must have gained some knowledge. What knowledge did he gain?

The Bible tells us that too. The instant he bites the fruit, he notices he is naked. Before that he had no idea he was naked. This just means he became self-conscious. Before that, he had no self-consciousness, and he had no idea even what naked was. Now, Adam has come to believe that he is a discrete thing; this is the birth of self-consciousness. He became aware of himself as separate.

Immediately, from the first nibble, he is cast out of the Garden into the world of suffering. And, from that moment on, he is trying to get back in to the Garden, where he is complete and whole, and lacks nothing.

If that story is true, then it must have something to do with you. So then, what? When you come out of the womb (which you can't remember but you can see in a baby), you have no idea that you are separate. A baby is just purely aware. How would a baby know it has a body? How would it know it has a head? Or two eyes? If a baby looked in a mirror, would it know that the image is of itself? This concept needs to be taught, no? It is just an image, an image appearing.

The baby has no idea its mother is separate because it has no idea that it is separate. If it doesn't know that it is separate, then it doesn't know that anything is separate from it. It has not yet bitten the fruit from the tree of knowledge. All there is, is knowing, not knowledge, information, or concept; not knowing what something is. Simply knowing, here and now, which is synonymous with aware. Aware equals knowing, in my usage.

A baby does not know that it exists separately because there is no sense of self yet. However, immediately, your mother starts calling you by your name, saying, "Good baby," etc. But how, at first, would a baby know that a sound is its name? How would it even know it is a name, or even a word? It is just an aural experience. A baby doesn't even know it is a sound, it's just something happening.

When a baby comes out of the womb, what is present is the basic operating system, as in a computer—the five senses and consciousness. There is no actual, mental data as of yet programmed into the hard drive, the brain. (Yes, there may be some seed impressions from inside the womb, but for our purposes here, we can say that mind is empty when it comes out of the womb.)

So, your mother is calling your name over and over, and you are in the garden of non-separation, no self, and one day, after hearing this sound many times, it dawns on you, "Ah, I am Sal." This, which has no form, simply aware, makes a mistake and identifies with form. The Bible also speaks about this. It says that we are all born with original sin. This is very true. But, it is completely misunderstood.

The Hebrew word sin means, "missing the mark." It is not "being bad" or "doing evil." Original sin is just the original error of judgment, or mistake. What we do with the original mistake or misidentification is say, "Ah, I am Sal." And, immediately, mother is separate, and world is separate because now, "I am separate." This is when "you," this ego/self, were born. It probably happens within the first few months after coming out of the womb.

From the first mistake, or identifying of the formless with form, impressions are recorded in the mind and this is the creation of the belief in self. You are born into a particular culture, in a particular time to particular parents and because of those arbitrary occurrences and your identification with them, you come to believe that that particular set of impressions is who you are.

By the time you are an adult, this self/ego seems like quite a formidable fortress, doesn't it? It seems solid and real, complex and confusing. Then, when you get on the spiritual path, you hear that you need to kill this self and that it may take fifty lifetimes to do so. Well, if you did have to dismantle and destroy all of that data, it probably would take fifty lifetimes because, by the time you are an adult, there are billions of pieces of data in there.

Clearly, if you were born in Saudi Arabia, you would have a completely different set of impressions in your brain and think that is who you are. But the date, time and place of our birth are really arbitrary and just the way it happened. Since we identify with the original sin, we identify with the impressions built upon it. So then, how essentially true can this particular set of impressions be?

In truth, this formidable ego that you need to kill and that seems so imposing is like a house of cards. The first card is the belief in self and all of the other cards are built on top of that. What we are doing with the three carousels of mind—psychology, philosophy and spirituality—is just moving cards around, rearranging, or trying to remove them all one by one.

It is endless. But what happens if you just remove the first card? What happens to the whole pile? It collapses upon itself.

That is what we are doing here, removing the first card. And in removing that first card, we come to see something different than we have seen before, something that is essential and always present. We see this sense of self that we think we have had our whole life is not solid. It is just like any other appearance—a sound, a thought, a vision, an experience—it comes and goes. Since that is true, then, for someone who is ready, it can't be as difficult to deal with as we have been told. We will look into this in more depth in the inquiries, and you will see for yourself.

You could say you are coming back home to the free, untainted aware that was present prior to identifying with the body and personality as who you are. As a newborn is aware without any conception of or identification with a notion of I, your natural default condition is aware. And no "I" or ego is required for that to be known.

PART 1

PART ONE — INQUIRIES AND EXPERIMENTS

Please read the inquiries with care and in no rush. If an inquiry is not clear to you, it is best to stick with it until it is. Go slowly, reread segments, and whole inquiries. Do the experiments until they are clear for you. This is not a novel, a spiritual philosophy book, or a story meant for entertainment. It is a means of inquiry for you to have a shift of knowing and to allow your mind to be finished seeking. If you just read it and collect some concepts, it won't work, it will just be more philosophy.

You are going to start to see something different than you have known before. Don't worry about where it is leading; just go step-by-step and see if what is being shared in each inquiry is true. If it is, you will know.

INQUIRY ONE — YOUR ESSENTIAL BEING

The foundation of this work is a clear recognition of your "essential being." This is a shift of knowing—from falsely believing yourself to be limited to or located within this body/mind organism, to coming to know your essential being of freedom. Taking a moment to recognize this is what I call having a "holiday." We have them throughout the inquiries. You will see what a holiday is as we proceed. When you see the symbol:

⁓⦅⟡⦆⁓

This is an indication to stop reading and have a short break to recognize what has just been shared. What you recognize in a holiday is your essential being. At first, you may not realize that, but it will become more and more obvious as we proceed.

It is not about understanding what has just been said, it is about seeing whether it is true or not. I ask you to have many holidays throughout the book. This work is not about mental intelligence; it is about recognizing something very clearly, again and again, and seeing more and more the implication of what you recognize. A holiday is the recognition.

Keep your eyes open during holidays unless there is an experiment where I ask you to close them. All the senses should be functioning. We are not trying to get into a meditative state, slow down the mind, or anything like that. Whatever is, is fine—thoughts, no thoughts, sensations or sounds. Be relaxed, not stiff. If you need to scratch your nose or whatever, it is no problem.

Experiment — Attention is Free

Now, in a very easeful way, relax the focus of attention. Don't focus on any one thing, so that you are not attending to anything in particular, like thoughts, sensations, or anything in your visual environment. Just for a moment, relax the focus of attention and allow attention to be open and free. This is having a holiday.

Please do this now for a moment, maybe a few seconds, or longer if it happens naturally. Eyes open.

Attention is a function, completely natural. We need it for our work, driving, or doing whatever we are doing. But just for a moment, here, once again relax attention, allow it to be unfocused on anything in particular, allow it to be free. (You are aware of the visual environment, but you are not focusing the eyesight on any particular object.) Please have a holiday again now and do this.

⁂

Notice that attention is free, it moves freely—goes to a sound, a thought, a sensation, etc. If you are relaxing the focus of attention and then you notice that you are attending to something in particular, like thoughts, no problem. When you do recognize that you are attending, once again relax and allow attention to be free. Do this for a few moments. (To relax the focus of attention does not mean that you don't see, hear or feel, it just means that you are not attending to any one thing in particular.) Please have a holiday now and relax the focus of attention for a few moments.

⁂

When you relax the focus of attention, you will notice something—you are aware. I am not talking about a state of awareness, or awareness as an object that I am aware of. Just very simple and ordinary—aware. Not aware of any one thing in particular, just aware. Very ordinary, no big deal. Prior to focusing on something (thought, a sound, an object) you are aware, and then when you put attention on something, you are aware of that thing. But, prior to focusing, you are simply present aware. Have a holiday now for a moment to notice this.

❧

If you focus on a particular object, like thoughts, then yes, you are aware of thoughts. That's very natural. When you notice that, just relax the focus and allow attention to be free. Then notice you are aware, not of anything in particular, simply aware. (Objects, thoughts and sensations are all present in aware, but you do not pause and focus on any of them.) This is a holiday. Please do this, now.

❧

This is very simple and ordinary, nothing is going to happen, but you will see where it leads if you follow along. If this is clear so far, then move on. If not, please go back and go through it again.

Experiment — Focused Attention

Go slowly and intently through these and all of the experiments. Take your time. See what is being pointed to.

Using a little intention, focus on something—thoughts, or if there are no thoughts, then some physical sensation. When you do this, recognize that when attention is focused on one object in particular, you are aware of that object, exclusively. Now, focus on one thing to the exclusion of everything else. Take a moment to do this for a little while with your eyes closed and then open your eyes.

Now, with your eyes open, have a holiday, relax the focus of attention. You see that aware was exclusive when focused on one object. Now see, aware is all-inclusive. The words on this page, all of the objects in the room, the sounds, the sensations of your body—are all included in aware. If you look out the window, everything you see, everything you hear, everything you smell exists within aware—everything. Take a moment to see this, now.

There is often the tendency to think in a dualistic way—there is me and my awareness and everything appears in my awareness. That puts you into a subject-object paradigm, which, in itself, creates a sense of separation. There is not a "me" and "my awareness," there is simply aware.

For a moment, let go of the notion of a separate "I." See this, now.

❧

Notice something else. When attention is not focused on anything in particular, you can see that aware is not attached or bound to anything. So, you can say it is free. Have a holiday and see this.

❧

So far, when we have a holiday, we recognize that what is, is aware, all-inclusive and free. (Part of what's occurring is we are dropping the notion of an "I" centrally located somewhere in this body/mind. What's left is simply aware.)

Is this all very clear? Go through this experiment again if it is not completely clear.

Experiment — Visual

Looking straight ahead, just using your visual sense, notice everything is included within aware; everything exists within aware. Have a look and notice this for a moment, now.

In this next section, the inquiry is directed to help you see what is when identification with the body is dropped. This will set the stage for another recognition coming up. Continuing to look straight ahead, notice that somewhere in your lower peripheral vision are included two colored objects. (I am referring to your legs, but now forget that I said that.) They are just particular shapes and colors. Now, without using your mind at all, not using memory, or any knowledge of what those objects are, just here and now, in your direct peripheral visual experience...

Do those objects say, "my legs" or are they simply some objects with particular shapes and colors? Have a look and see, now.

If you say, "my legs," then you are obviously using your mental knowledge, memory. Without using your mind to define them, they are just shapes and colors amongst many other shapes and colors, appearing in aware. In fact, without using thought, you could not call them, "my legs" at all. Take a moment now and see this.

Make sure this experiment is clear before moving on.

Experiment — No Head

Now, keeping your eyes straight ahead, and without using your imagination or memory, in your own direct visual experience here and now, do you have a head? Take a moment to look.

What proof or evidence, in your own direct visual experience right now, indicates that there is a head? There might be a little bit of vague shaped color in your view. But does that say nose? Take a moment to look.

And furthermore, in your own direct experience right now, do you have two eyes? Or is there just open space? Without using memory, only in your direct visual experience here and now, can you say you have two eyes? Look and see, now.

❦

Please spend ample time with this experiment. It needs to be clearly seen.

❦

When you came out of the womb, how could you have known that you have two eyes? Or a head or a body? You hadn't acquired that knowledge yet. All a baby knows, and not by means of words or description, but, in its own direct experience, is: aware, all-inclusive. If you pointed a mirror at a baby, how would it know that that image is its own, if it has not yet come to know it has a body, that it is separate? This has to be taught to a baby.

A baby has no sense of "I." It is simply aware. There is no notion, "This is my hand, that is my mother," there is simply aware. It is not until impressions are recorded in the brain that the notion of "I" is created. If, right now, you let go of the notion of "I," what is present (or remains) is aware.

❦

Right now, in your direct experience, there are shapes and colors, but without the knowledge of what those are, can you say you have a head or a body? Look and see.

❦

If you say you have a head, then you are obviously using memory, thoughts. So, be clear, in your own direct visual experience only, right now, do you have a head?

Please make sure this is very clear before continuing. Go through it again and make sure it is. This is leading somewhere, so it is important to see it clearly.

❦

Experiment — Sensations

For this experiment you will close your eyes after you read the following instructions.

Within this all-inclusiveness of aware, there are some sensations. For example, the butt on the chair. (Now, forget those words.) If you just look at that sensation, in your own direct knowing, now, without using your knowledge of what it is, does that sensation say, "butt-on-chair?" Or is it just a sensation appearing, along with everything else, in aware?

Now, please close your eyes and do that experiment for a while. See what is being shared. Do this with other sensations as well. What this is pointing to is that everything exists within aware. All your body sensations, all your visual and audio input, the body itself, all the objects in the room, all the objects in the sky, everything—it all exists in aware.

❦

Again, with your eyes closed, look at all the sensations appearing. See that without using your memory, they do not say, "my body." You need to use your mind to put those sensations together as "my body." Without using your mind, as in memory and fantasy, aren't these just sensations appearing within aware? Do they say, "my body?" Take a moment here to recognize this.

❦

Now, do the experiment with your eyes open. There are also sights and sounds as well. They are all included in aware, including the sensations of the so-called body. Do any of the sensations say, "my body?"

Do this experiment until it is very clear. Please make sure it is because it leads into the next experiment.

❦

Aware

Looking again, now. Can you deny that you are aware? Don't get philosophical here. Be simple. Ordinary, everyday aware. Can you deny that you are aware?

Ignore this body and mind. When you do so, see that you cannot deny the fact that you are aware. It is perfectly obvious, self-evidently so. Have a holiday now and see this.

❦

Does aware require any supportive evidence to be known, like thought, memory, fantasy or any information at all? Anything other than itself? Or is it just directly known? Clearly evident. Self-evidently so.

When a baby comes out of the womb, it is aware. That is all it knows. It doesn't know words or descriptions, but it is aware. It has no idea what any objects are, not even its own hands or bodily sensations. There is only aware, or knowing, with no descriptive knowledge.

❧

Please go back and repeat these last few experiments and make sure they are very clear before continuing.

❧

Self-Knowing Aware

This, which is aware, knows itself. It is not a subject-object knowing, like the observer seeing a tree. It does not require knowledge or memory. Aware knows itself with no thought or understanding needed, it simply knows itself. If this is not clear, we can take another approach.

Another name for aware is knowing. Look around the room you are in. There is a knowing within which this room exists. Take a moment now and recognize this knowing. (pause) You could move into, "I know this room," but that puts you in subject-object duality. That is not what I am pointing at. For a moment, drop the I, and what is left is knowing. Have a holiday and see this.

❧

Experiment — Inside Outside

Is there an inside and an outside? What we have come to believe is that I am in here, a soul or a self, aware of things out there. However, is there a line where you end and the world begins, or is there just one seamless whole, aware? Do you stop at the skin line? Have a look.

❧

There is no line here indicating inside and outside. Everything that seems to exist as an inside or outside exists within aware. There is just one seamless whole—aware. Everything that exists in the entire universe, exists in aware.

Again, I am not saying everything exists in your awareness, that's subject (your) and object (awareness) duality and makes awareness a thing that contains stuff. Rather, we are looking to recognize that aware simply is, knowing simply is.

Take a moment to recognize that aware knows itself. Please be very clear about this before proceeding.

A SHIFT OF KNOWING

This recognition is the most important one to see clearly. This is where the assumption of who you are as limited and exclusive can shift. Take plenty of time to see this clearly. Don't rush through this experiment, see it again. Without this being clear, the rest of the work will not be effective.

Inquiry — Who am I?

You can say, "I am aware," right? Don't get philosophical here. Just be simple. I am aware. Look and see.

❦

Now, look at it in a different way.

You are not "doing aware" or "being aware."

In fact, you are not separate from aware.

Who you are, essentially, is aware.

Before, during, and after all thoughts, feelings, sensory objects, and experiences—**YOU ARE**.

All those appearances come and go, and yet, you are here always—**AWARE**.

Throughout your whole life, with all of the changes in your mind, body, and circumstances, you have been here, **AWARE**.

If this is true, and you see this for yourself, who must you be essentially?

AWARE is your essential being, it is **YOU**.

See this again. Look.

You are not "doing aware" or "being aware."

In fact, you are not separate from aware.

Who you are, essentially, is aware.

Aware is your essential being.

Take plenty of time with this inquiry until it is clear.

❧

Normally, when we say, "I am aware," we think of ourselves as the noun "I" doing something, like being aware. This is the basis of duality, the "I" doing aware, or the "I" being aware of an object. Ignore the notion of the limited "I" located here, somewhere in this body, and recognize that what you are is aware. Your essential being is aware. (Your essential being is not the separate sense or feeling of "I," your essential being is "aware.") The proof of that for yourself is that you are aware of the sense of I.

Relax the focus of attention from the contracted feeling of "I" and allow attention to be free and open. Ignore this body and mind. See that what you are in essence is aware. Please do this now for a moment with eyes open.

❧

This does not take any knowledge, memory, or identification with body or mind. It is self-evident, not subject-object. Simply, here and now, aware is my essential being, before, during, and after all appearances. It needs no mental support and is perfectly obvious. Have a holiday and see this.

❧

See if this is true or not. I am not saying you are awareness, as awareness can be considered an object. I am saying that who you are is aware. Your nature is aware. You = aware. You (aware) are directly known unto yourself, without the need of any mind, knowledge, fantasy, or ideas. You (aware) are self-evidently known to yourself. Have a holiday and see this, now.

❧

You are not a thing. You are aware. And within you/aware, all the objects are included. Sensory objects, mental and emotional objects, physical objects, and experiences are all included in you, aware.

You are not within this body. This body is an appearance within you, aware.

Is this true? Look.

❧

Experiment — You are Free

Have a holiday now and relax the focus of attention.

Is aware bound to anything? Is it attached? Or is it free?

Since aware is your essential being, then your essential being is free. You are free, here and now.

Take a moment to see this for yourself.

Isn't this how a baby is when it comes out of the womb? A baby doesn't know it has a head and a body, or that its mother is separate. All a baby knows is freely aware (not that it knows it intellectually, but it is a knowing, which is synonymous with aware). Isn't it the same now for you as it was when you were a baby? Who you are, essentially, is aware. This body, this mind, this personality, which you have mistakenly identified with, exists within aware.

You lose the sense of your essential free nature when you bite the fruit from the tree of knowledge and believe, "I am this body/mind." It is this notion of duality, subject/object, that creates this sense of a separate me that is bound.

Again, have a holiday and see–I am aware of myself, not myself as a physical or mental object, but simply, self-evidently aware. A knowing that is not knowledge, but is simply known, here and now. Aware. This is who I am.

Now that we have come to recognize a few things, see for yourself if the following is true about whom you are, your essential being.

You are:

Aware — Have a holiday and see if this is true.

All-Inclusive — Have a holiday and see if this is true.

Free — Have a holiday and see if this is true.

~~~

As you can see, none of these can be objectified, as in a thing that you are, they are simply what is true about your essential being.

~~~

Not Special

Because of all the ideas we have collected about what so-called enlightenment will look or feel like, it is very easy to doubt that this very simple and ordinary recognition can be what we have been seeking. It is not what you expected. Who you are is very ordinary and very simple. The more you recognize this, the more the profound implications of this recognition will be known. For now, just stay with the inquiry and you will see where it leads.

~~~

Being in the Now

We hear that we need to be in the now, or in the present moment. Is it possible to be anywhere other than now? Whether you know it or not, or whether you think you are lost in the past or future, in fact, you are always now. There is no other possibility.

Have a holiday and look. Now is another name for you. You are always now. You are not in the now.

∽⁊∾

Have a holiday and look. Who I am—aware, all-inclusive, free, now. See this!

∽⁊∾

This is a shift of knowing. Nothing special happens. This will become more clear and doubtless as you go through the inquiries.

What a Holiday Is

By continuing to have holidays and seeing this again and again, the mind can become liberated from beliefs and the so-called bondage to self. What we are doing is coming to the end of seeking and becoming. We are not attaining a new state of awareness or anything like that.

It is important to say here that you are not trying to get into a state where you are always freely aware, or unfocused on anything in particular. That is a Buddhist teaching and practice, but it is not what we are doing. We are just, for a moment, having a holiday from our beliefs and identifications to see what is our essential being, that is all. A few seconds is enough.

Holidays happen spontaneously. They happen spontaneously for everyone, every day. We are mostly unaware when it happens. Now, we are simply being consciously aware of it, for the purpose of noticing something.

A holiday reveals the natural default human condition, which is free, here and now. Because there is not this knowing when holidays normally happen, and we hardly even notice when they do, they have no ability to liberate. Know what is true and this knowing is what will set you free.

Now, when a holiday happens, the natural default human condition, notice something—**I am aware, all-inclusive, free, now.**

See this again and again. This can liberate you from identification with ego/self, and end seeking and becoming.

⁂

Remember, focused attention is natural and necessary, so don't try to hold on to a state of awareness. Be natural. But, during the day, whenever it naturally occurs to you to have a holiday, just relax the focus of attention and know—I am aware and free, here and now.

⁂

I heartfully suggest going back now to page 31, **Inquiries and Experiments**, and read through and do the experiments up to here again before continuing. It will become clearer if you do so and it is essential for this to be known before moving forward.

After doing that, my suggestion is to stop here for now. Over the next few days, have holidays. Holidays happen spontaneously. Also, sit for five or ten minutes a day and have holidays. When a holiday happens, recognize what you have come to know. Then, in a few days, go through the previous experiments again. Do this several times, in fact. Once everything is very clear, proceed to the next Inquiry.

You may be tempted to disregard my suggestion to wait a few days and re-read, and instead, just plow on through. It is a bad idea. If you rush through this Inquiry without taking time, it won't do its work. There is no rush, and everything needs to be very clear. This is about coming to the end of seeking forever, so be clear and thorough.

❧❧❧

Already Free

If you took a few days off and re-read and looked into the first inquiry, and you are clear about what is being shared, you can move on to the next inquiry. Again, this will not work if you move on without recognizing what has been pointed to so far.

We are not trying to get into a state of always being unfocused aware. When you have a holiday, just for a moment, see what is true. Then if you go right back into focusing on something, no problem, it's natural. Doing whatever you are doing, notice, just for a moment—I am aware, free.

Have a holiday, now. Don't attend to anything in particular. It's very natural for attention to go to a thought after a few seconds. No problem. As soon as you notice, again, relax the focus of attention. Do this now.

When you relax attention, see that what is, is aware, all-inclusive, and free, now. Your essential being is aware, all-inclusive and free. See this again.

Although words are need for guidance, they are not to be held onto. It is having holidays and recognizing your essential being that reveals liberation.

If you see that this is true, then now, you know. It's not a big experience or state. We go one step at a time.

Knowing is not separate from aware, this knowing is aware. I use the words "knowing" and "aware" synonymously. Know what is true and see: I am already free. Have a holiday and see this.

Your essential being, which is free, is very ordinary and obvious. But we have been taught or have read something different—that your essential being is a deep or big experience, and that it is very difficult and rare to attain. Why would your nature (who you are) be anything other than obvious and ordinary? We are not trying to come upon or attain something new.

What we are doing is recognizing something that is already true, and this will help free the mind of seeking and becoming. We are freeing this mind of the nonsense we have been taught to believe. The end of seeking is synonymous with liberation. The value of this will become more and more apparent as we proceed.

❧

Have a holiday. See the difference when attention is focused and when it is unfocused. Exclusive, then all-inclusive.

❧

Jumping Off

When attention is focused on one object, you could say that aware is bound to an object. (That is not actually true, but see what I mean anyway.) Then, when attention relaxes, you see that aware is free—freely aware. What is here is free already. You are this. Take a moment to see this, now.

❦

What we have been trying to do on the path is make a "self" free. We spend years trying to do that in meditation and with other methods. We think, "I, this ego/self, needs to be free." But what we have not done in all our spiritual practices is to have this shift of knowing, to see that I am already free. For a moment, ignore this body/mind, ignore thoughts and see that what is here, aware and free, is who I am.

By doing this, you are jumping off the belief in self and the carousels of mind, and knowing your essential, free nature.

Jump off!

❦

Holidays

When holidays happen, it is not enough just to get some relief or to relax from focused attention for a moment. That does not liberate. When a holiday happens, know—I am not attached to this body/mind; I am free, aware; this is my nature, this is who I am. This knowing is what can liberate the mind from ignorance and misidentification and can lead to the end of seeking. You do not need to change this form, mentally, emotionally, or physically. Leave that all alone, and see what is true already.

❦

A Story

Moses goes up to the top of the mountain. When he gets there, he meets God and asks, "Sir, what is your name?" And God says, "I am that I am." If you have a holiday now, can you not also say and see, "I am that I am?" Of course, you can. Was God telling Moses who God is or was he trying to tell Moses who Moses is?

I know that I am. Since I am not an object, I can't say I know what I am, but I cannot deny that I am. If I say I am a thing, I must be referring to this body or to thoughts. If I say I am awareness, I am making awareness into a thing.

In fact, I am no-thing—simply aware, free and all-inclusive. Those words speak of my nature, they do not describe an object. I am, but I am no-thing in particular. God was saying to Moses: "Have a shift of knowing."

⁓

Self

Is self, or ego, a real object? Has it been here your whole life? Let's find out.

Self is another word for ego, as in the sense of self. It is identifying with this form, body, and thought impressions as who I am. For example, identifying with my past personal history, future desires, beliefs, cultural conditionings, and so on. In many non-dual teachings, we are supposed to kill or get rid of the self/ego. We need to find out about self, see what it actually implies and then see what needs to be done.

Experiment — Focus on self

Focus on a specific thought or a sensation that makes you feel there is a "me," self, here. Close your eyes and see that when you do that it is very limiting, exclusive, even claustrophobic. Spend a few moments doing this now, and after you have had that feeling, open your eyes again.

Do you see how limiting that feels?

Now, relax the focus of attention and see the difference. Not limited, but free.

༺⚜༻

No self

When you come out of the womb, there is no sense of self yet. You have not yet bitten into the fruit from the tree of knowledge. That knowledge is self-consciousness. But, after a few months of hearing a name called, you say, "Aha, I am (your name)." This is your first birth of self.

We think that this sense of self has been here our whole lifetime. By the time we are an adult, and even much sooner, we believe that this is an empirical fact. Then you hear that you have to kill the ego and it might take you many lifetimes because ego is a very formidable object.

In truth, this sense of self is just an appearance, like any other appearance. It comes and goes many times each day. You can already see that there are many times each day when you are not focused on "me." What is present is aware, even when there is no sense of self appearing. Freely aware is the default human condition, like when you came out of the womb. Many times each day, you take a birth of self. It is not just the one birth you took when you were an infant. This sense of self comes and goes, just as any other thought or appearance does. Just like a wave in the ocean. See this for yourself over the course of your days.

These moments of unfocused attention, in themselves, won't help liberate the mind. What liberates is knowing that you are free. When a holiday happens, know what is true—here and now, my essential being is free.

This so-called self doesn't actually exist as a discrete, empirical object. In truth, there is no actual self. Because of this sense of self, this "me" feeling, we believe that self/ego is solid and empirical. We don't realize it is just an assumption we have come to accept. We simply take it for granted without actually looking into it to see if it is true. Now, we are seeing something different—I am freely aware, and I take many so-called births of self, each day.

Not only is the *feeling* of me considered self, but my particular personal history, beliefs, future goals, and desires seem to indicate that there is a solid empirical self here, and that this is who I am. But is any of this true, now? Aren't these all changing appearances that come and go?

Taking births is fine, it is natural. We are not trying to kill the ego here. We are just coming to see what is true, what is essential, and how we operate.

Santa Claus

Up until the age of seven or so, you took for granted that there is a Santa Claus. You didn't have any evidence of this, but you believed it, unquestioningly. Then one day, you came to know that there is no Santa Claus and that belief was gone. You don't have to keep looking up the chimney to see if Santa Claus is there, you just know. It is the same with what we are doing here. Know what is true, and in that knowing, the belief in an empirical self is over. You don't have to be on holiday all day to know what is true. You come to know, and it is over.

That is what self-inquiry is—knowing what is true and seeing more and more how we operate from this belief in self. The natural default human condition is free. We default to this many times each day. Now, when it happens, I say, notice—I am free.

Knowing Who I am is Not an Experience

Experiences come and go, but who you are is not an experience. Who you are is knowing/aware. Taking a birth of self is an experience. That is why spiritual experiences are not what we are looking for. They occur in this, aware, who I am, and they come and go, just like every other experience. We think that a spiritual experience will happen, last forever and that will be enlightenment. But no, that spiritual experience is no more enlightenment than any other experience. All experiences come and go, and yet I remain the same, before, during, and after—aware and free.

Look and see this, now.

Holidays Happen Spontaneously

The moment you notice that you are attending exclusively to thoughts, it is a holiday. There is no doing a holiday. The recognition that you are attending to an object means the holiday is happening. Notice how this happens without your doing.

It doesn't matter if you are lost in thoughts for an hour or a day. Why? Because whether you are lost in the thoughts or not, the truth is, you are free. You know this because the moment a holiday happens you see that it is still true, always. We see, again and again—I am free. Have a holiday and know this.

❦

Knowing is What Liberates

What liberates is not a holiday, what liberates is knowing when a holiday happens. Know once and for all:

- **Aware is here and now** — Now you know.
- **Aware includes everything** — Now you know.
- **Aware is free** — Now you know.
- **Aware is not separate from who I am** — Now you know.
- **My essential being is aware** — Now you know.
- **When a holiday happens, know** — This is who I am.

This is already liberation.

We are not going to attain liberation in the future, we are seeing what is already true; my natural human condition is

free already. I just didn't know it before. Have a holiday and
see it now.

❧

Purifying Your Mind

They say you need to purify yourself, so you'll be ready to
receive enlightenment, or merge with the divine. Supposedly,
you need to purify the mind of vasanas (tendencies), karmas,
and all of that. Once you purify your mind enough, then you'll
be ready to recognize what's true. This mind is never going to
be pure, how could it? It's got a lifetime of billions of pieces of
information; how are you going to get rid of them all? Forget
it, it's impossible. But, what is pure already? Let's have a look.
Have a holiday, now.

❧

Here and now, you know who you are, right? Aware.

Is there even a speck of dust on who you are? Have a holiday
and see.

❧

Mind, body, impressions, and thoughts are not pure. This body/mind is the experiencing mechanism of life. It gets dinged, knocked, and hit—emotionally, psychologically, and physically. It has bruises, it's natural. That's not going to be purified in the way you have come to believe. Have a holiday again. Look, now.

❦

If you recognize your essential being, you recognize that you are pure already. The idea of purifying this form is false. In truth, see for yourself, you are already pure.

If you identify yourself as this body/mind organism, you will say, "I've got to purify 'me.'" However, your nature is already pure, spotless and stainless, with not a speck of dust on it. Is it true? Have a holiday and see.

It is having holidays and recognizing your essential being that reveals liberation. Don't make a thing out of these words. Drop the words and see what is.

❦

We've been told we've got to purify this form to know truth, to awaken, or to get enlightened. That's not true. The only thing you need to do is see what's already pure. It has always been pure. This is where you live. You can stop purifying this body/mind organism, let it be as it is. A used car is not going to look like a new car, is it? Why would an old human being look like a new human being? See if this is true.

Now that we have come to recognize some more things, see for yourself if the following is true about who you are, your essential being.

You are:

Aware — Have a holiday and see if this is true.

All-Inclusive — Have a holiday and see if this is true.

Free — Have a holiday and see if this is true.

Now — Have a holiday and see if this is true.

No self — Have a holiday and see if this is true.

Pure — Have a holiday and see if this is true.

As you can see, none of these can be objectified, as in a thing that you are. They are simply what is true about your essential being.

You are Always Here

You have been told on the path that it will take you thirty years of meditation and quieting your mind, and then maybe, you will come to know who you are, if you are lucky. I was a hardcore meditator and I must have been pretty bad at it because I could never still the thoughts for more than a brief amount of time. But, in truth, how much time does it take to know what is already true? Have a holiday and look.

⁓

It takes no time because what is true is already true, now. We are not gaining something new, like a new consciousness or state, or enlightenment. We have just never noticed before what has always been true.

⁓

I Haven't Changed

An interesting thing happened to me when I first began spiritual seeking in 1998. I was sitting on a bus back to New York, returning from meeting a teacher. It was my first time ever meeting a teacher. I was sitting on the bus and all of a sudden, something unusual happened. I started going back through my life and seeing that in each moment of my life, I was here. I saw myself in many different circumstances and environments. I saw that even back to the age of seven, I had never changed, even though all of my thoughts, emotions, experiences, circumstances, and the body itself had changed, constantly. Yet, I had not changed even one iota. I was the same one looking through these eyes in each moment.

I then went forward in my life to the age of ninety, and I saw that even when this body is very old, I am the same. The body is in constant change, and so are the circumstances, beliefs, and emotions. Yet I had not changed at all.

It was a profound experience, which I chalked off to a peculiar experience and thought, "Well, that was interesting." I didn't have anyone to explain to me what I recognized, and I wasn't ready for it to liberate me from seeking. What was revealed was true. Years later, after I was finished, I remembered that experience and knew what was revealed.

EXPERIMENT—Go Back Through Your Life

Let's do a little experiment to see this for ourselves. I'd like you to pick a specific incident from your life in the not too distant past, perhaps from this year. Imagine yourself in that circumstance and while you're there, recall the sights, sounds, and people that were there as much as possible. Put yourself there, see out of those eyes.

Take a moment here to do this.

Now, if I had come around and tapped you on the shoulder and said, "Have a holiday," what would be here? Aware, free, all-inclusive, right? Any different than aware, free, all-inclusive, now?

Have a look now and see. You have to take the time to do this so that it is clear to you.

❧

Now, go back ten or twenty years; pick another circumstance and do the same thing. Imagine the sights, sounds, and people that were around. Put yourself there and see out of those eyes. Take some time to do this; you have to put yourself in that circumstance to recognize what is pointed to. Do this now.

❧

If you had a holiday then, what would be here?

Who I am, aware, free, all-inclusive, pure, now. Is this any different from what is here, now? See for yourself.

❧

Go back to a young childhood experience and do the same thing. Please take the time to do this now.

❦

If you were to have had a holiday then, what would be there? Wouldn't it be the same aware, free, all-inclusive as is here now?

Your body is very different today, isn't it? If you haven't changed, and yet your body has changed over these years, and your thoughts and beliefs have changed, how can you be this body or the content of this mind?

It's not even the same body. Science tells us that every fifteen years or so, a majority of the cells in your body have been replaced. The bones are the slowest, they take about fifteen years. But, in fifteen years, the bones won't be the same bones they were fifteen years ago. You will have a completely different body. And yet you haven't changed at all, have you?

What about when you're ninety years old? How different will your body be then from when you were two years old, and yet can you see that you will be same?

You don't change, do you? You haven't changed at all, have you? Often, older people say, "I still feel the same as I did when I was a kid." Yes, because you are the same. The body is getting older, but you haven't changed. They don't know what it's pointing to, they just say, "I still feel young."

You haven't changed at all, have you? In your whole life, all the forms and appearances and experiences have changed, but you, you haven't changed. You have always been aware, free and all-inclusive. Know this now!

⚬⚬✦⚬⚬

Please do the above experiment and make sure you clearly see what is being pointed to. Take your time going through it.

INQUIRY ONE: QUESTIONS AND ANSWERS

Intellectual Understanding and Past Experiences

> *Inquirer: I have an intellectual understanding and I know I think too much. I had a near death experience at one point in my life and aware was very clear. Because of our conversations I discount it, but it continuously comes up. I wonder if I have to experience a certain thing, or if my mind is waiting for something.*

Salvadore (Sal): There are two things here that we need to look into: Intellectual understanding and valuing a past experience. This experience you had in the past, where is it now?

> *Inquirer: Just in my mind.*

Sal: The actual experience, where is it, now?

> *Inquirer: It's not here.*

Sal: That's right. What is here is a memory of something that happened in the so-called past and you consider it to be special, important, profound, and meaningful. We have to stop doing that.

> **Inquirer:** *What I got out of the first session was that experiences are just stories.*

Sal: When they are happening they are true, in the sense that they are happening. After the fact, there is no truth to them, they are illusion, fantasy. That experience will never happen again, whether you want it to or not. No experience repeats itself. We are absolutely not in any way trying to achieve that or any other experience. This really has to be reckoned with. I know the temptation. We need to face the fact that we still believe liberation has something to do with experience—that I need to be in a particular experience or that some experience is going to come and blow my head off forever.

That is absolutely not what we are doing here. In fact, if you do have one of those experiences, it is going to be very difficult to wake up because it will be so infatuating that you will get lost thinking about it, thinking it means something, and then clinging on to it, hoping it will happen again because you think it is very special. What we are doing is not special at all.

When I say liberation is ordinary, I mean it. It is simply the natural human condition, now. Since that is true, then what is so special about some experience? Liberation is not an experience; it is just ordinary consciousness, free, now. It is the end of seeking. It is whatever is appearing, now. It could be anger, sadness, joy, peace, or whatever. No matter what is appearing now, it is true, isn't it? You can't deny it because here it is.

Because we read all these books that tell us, "Thou shalt not be angry, thou shalt be in a state of bliss and equanimity," we think there is something wrong with us when so-called negative things appear. The truth is, there is anger appearing. Why argue with it and say it is wrong? Because that is what we are taught to do—that we are wrong for having anger and right for having bliss. But neither is right or wrong; if they are present, then that is what is.

Stop reminiscing about that past. I don't reminisce at all because to me, nostalgia and reminiscing are suffering. We are longing for something that was so great, something that was then but isn't now, so obviously our current experience is inferior or lacking.

> **Inquirer:** *I think I am comparing what I am supposed to be looking for with that.*

Sal: Comparing your current experience with some past experience that you cherish, or some future possibility you imagine, is comparing what is actually true to some fantasy. What is true is right now, isn't it?

What we do is seek something other than what is right now. In this case, something transcendental. We are trying to become something other than what we are right now. Do you see this?

Inquirer: *Yes.*

Sal: Seeking for some great experience is becoming. Becoming something other than what I am, now. This is why it takes a great maturity to be finished. To be finished means all these games of seeking and becoming are over. If you say you want truth, then just look, here it is. You don't have to go anywhere or be anything different than you are, now.

Now, imagine yourself back in that experience. If I said to you, "Have a holiday," would you not be aware, all-inclusive, free, just as you are now?

Inquirer: *Yes.*

Sal: What I thought when those experiences happened to me, was that the experience was the thing I was looking for. (It's what we all think.) I thought that once I got some great experience like this that lasted forever, that would be it, I would be enlightened. What I failed to notice is that, in fact, I am aware of that experience. I never turned it around, so to speak, to know that.

What we are doing here is coming to know who I am, not what the experience is. What you recognize now, in a holiday, is what you would have recognized then in a holiday, if you had known to look. Here I am, aware, and this just happens to be the current experience.

The other thing you mentioned that we need to address is getting it intellectually.

Have a holiday. Don't focus on anything in particular, allow attention to be free. What is here is aware?

Inquirer: *Yes.*

Sal: Are you sure? Is it intellectual?

Inquirer: *Yes, I am sure, it is not intellectual.*

Sal: You just recognize, right? Thoughts are not needed for this are they?

Inquirer: No.

Sal: Because you are not focused on anything in particular, you see that everything is included here. Is this true?

Inquirer: Yes.

Sal: Is it true or is it intellectual?

Inquirer: It's true.

Sal: Looking now, if aware is not focused on anything in particular, you can say aware is unbound, or free. Is it true or intellectual?

Inquirer: It's true.

Sal: It is all very ordinary. Now, looking straight ahead, without using your memory or knowledge, can you say you have a head?

Inquirer: No.

Sal: Two little eyes?

Inquirer: No.

Sal: But, looking right now, can you deny you are aware?

Inquirer: No.

Sal: Is it intellectual?

Inquirer: No, it's true.

Sal: Right. This has nothing to do with thought. You just can't deny you are aware. Leave this body/mind behind, this which is aware is your nature, you are this which is aware. Is this clear?

Inquirer: Yes.

Sal: This is the most important thing to recognize. It is very simple but has to be recognized. I am aware, all-inclusive and free. Now, you see that this is not an intellectual understanding—it is a knowing. Do you see what I mean?

Inquirer: Yes.

Sal: These two things, holding on to past experiences and trying to understand intellectually, will keep you seeking. Maturity means to stop all of that and just see what is true, no thought, no past experience, simply see, now. This is jumping off the carousel of mind/self/ego.

The immature person wants to hold on to experience and understand. For you, who wants to be free, it is time to jump. Just this, what is, here and now.

❦

Feelings Accompanying Recognition

Inquirer: It seems that last week the recognition was so strong, and then over the week, it seems to have faded a little bit. Even when holidays happen, I can see, but it is not as vivid.

Sal: There isn't a strong, or not strong, recognition. There is just seeing what is true. But often, the first time someone recognizes this it can be surprising and may elicit some feelings. It is not always the case and it's not necessary. If that happened for you, then you may equate recognizing this with the feeling it elicited. And then when it doesn't happen again next time, you think that the recognition was not as "strong." What faded was the feeling it elicited. We are not looking for an experience of peace, bliss, or anything in particular. These things may accompany a recognition, but that is not a goal to look for, to always feel something nice.

What we are doing is coming to rest with what is. Being finished seeking, no matter what is appearing. Sometimes what is appearing is not pleasant. That is just the nature of this body/mind organism. Enlightened or not, you will not always experience good things. We are not trying to come into a new state where we feel relief and elation all the time.

What we are doing is coming to see what is true and being finished seeking and becoming anything other than what is. It is not a new state or feeling, it is very ordinary. Liberation is simply the natural human condition, free. We have gotten into a big mess in our minds, thinking there is something wrong with us and something has to be changed. But that is just because we have identified with the ever-changing mental and circumstantial appearances and we feel insecure and inadequate. We will see all of this very clearly in the coming inquiries, but have a holiday now, don't refer to this mind, and see that you are free already and that there is nothing to change.

⤫

What Is, Is—Unpleasant Experiences

Inquirer: *Last week, things weren't exactly fantastic. I ran into difficult family situations.*

Then I recognize, and I recognize, and I recognize, it's a vacillation and that in itself, is exhausting. I think, "I am back again... I am lost... then, here I am again." Just the fact of being more aware of it at this point, I think.

Sal: That's what it takes, especially in those trying times.

__Inquirer:__ But it is exhausting, and I think the fact that I realize that it's exhausting, that I recognize that I go back and forth so much, makes it worse.

Sal: Yes, and that's all fine too, it's natural. There's nothing wrong with that, so you don't have to think that there is. It's totally natural to do that. What we're doing here is coming to know what's true, not to get to a point where you never get into your thought processes or something like that. It's very natural, thoughts come up and attention will focus, especially compelling thoughts. Why wouldn't attention focus for a little while? We're not trying to get into a state where that is not happening.

__Inquirer:__ I realize that and that this whole thing is about the end of seeking.

Sal: Liberation is; it's your natural condition, isn't it?

Inquirer: *I just wish it stayed there.*

Sal: There's no "it" and no "there" to stay.

Inquirer: *I know, it comes and goes.*

Sal: Liberation doesn't come and go. Your essential being, who you are, free, is always the same. Thoughts come and go, situations come and go, experiences come and go, but you never come and go, do you?

We're coming to the end of thinking that there's anything wrong with you because of anything that appears. But if you fully believe the things that appear in your mind, then you get into these endless loops, over and over.

Inquirer: *Do you mean the stories I tell myself?*

Sal: Yes, but it doesn't mean unpleasant thoughts and feelings aren't going to appear. Why wouldn't they? Unpleasant circumstances happen. This body receives them and processes them and responds with thoughts and emotions. Why wouldn't that happen? It's natural. Getting in there and trying to solve it, resolve it, or get past the stories causes this looping, which is suffering.

Inquirer: I was going to say like a loop. Our brains are computers after all.

Sal: The brain is like a hard drive. It collects impressions—the impressions of your life and the impressions of your day. Impressions are recorded, and the mind just replays them as thoughts, emotions, or whatever. It is all very impersonal.

Inquirer: Yes, then we grasp on to those and make them our reality, and we get lost in our little stories.

Sal: That's suffering right there—creating stories that we believe are true. Liberation doesn't mean you won't have unpleasant experiences and thoughts, because you will, everyone does.

What we're doing again and again is recognizing, "I am free," that's all it is, "I am free." One day, it's finished for you. If something is pleasant, it's pleasant, and if something is not pleasant, it's not pleasant. You just stop arguing with it. Okay, it's unpleasant, that's what is.

Inquirer: When I have a holiday, the recognition, it's a relief and it's nice, but then I have this other little thing in my head and it's going, "But there's something that's bothering me, and I want to get back to that and think about it."

Sal: Exactly, that's right. The reason it compels you is that there's still a belief that there's some meaning and resolution in there. Why is that? Because that's what you've been trained to believe—psychology—that there's something in there that needs to be resolved. It's totally normal. You've been trained that way your whole life. Why wouldn't that continue for a while? It will, until it doesn't anymore. You know there's nothing to resolve in there. Give yourself a break with that one because it takes time. Recognizing what's true takes no time, but liberating this mind from that exact thing you said does take time because it's a habit, a whole lifetime of that habit. So, it's not even natural for it to end immediately.

When you find out that there's no Santa Claus it's easy, simple, and you never doubt it again. This is different because there is deep conditioning in the mind which says that you're supposed to resolve something in there. The way it works is coming to see, "I am free," again and again until it's doubtless, and then you don't need to see it ever again.

You know that there's no Santa Claus, you know you're free. You don't need to look up the chimney anymore to see that there's no Santa Claus, and you don't need to look to see who you are because you know, it's over. But that takes as long as it takes. It took time for me, and it takes time for everyone.

❦

Freedom is Already Here

Inquirer: You mentioned that it is the recognition that is the holiday, that's very important.

Sal: Exactly, because without the recognition, or knowing, a holiday doesn't do a thing. A holiday happens to everyone a hundred times a day, but it is useless without knowing who I am.

Inquirer: Yes, it was good you said that because it took me from making the whole holiday thing a process of, "Okay, recognize, have a holiday, all-inclusive...", to the simple fact that the very act of recognition is the holiday. It's just like, "Oh, wow."

Sal: Yes, and it's freedom already. It's not a goal. I don't want you to have a goal in mind that one of these days it's going to be over. It's not like that.

Have a holiday, right now.

❦

Sal: Here and now you're free? It is already over isn't it?

Inquirer: *Yes, it's nice.*

Sal: So where do you want to live?

Inquirer: *Here.*

Sal: Exactly. They say that you need to want liberation more than a drowning man wants air. There's no judgment here, but if you see that you're going into the mind and trying to resolve things, just know, in that moment, that's what you want. You don't want freedom because, if you want freedom, here it is. It's not a judgment, it's just something to see.

When we're lost in the mind and going over and over suffering, then we know that that's what we want in that moment. We want to just to get in there, to try to resolve something at the level of thought. If we want freedom as much as a drowning man wants air, here it is, always here.

❦

Unborn

Inquirer: Can you explain more about what you mean about being unborn?

Sal: Unborn is your nature. What is born is the original mistake, believing "I am separate." It happens first when you are a couple months old, and then it happens millions more times in your life. You identify with self, and then you default to the natural human condition, which is free. And that happens continuously.

We may not have noticed it before, but there are many times in each day when we are not identifying as a self, we are just freely aware. No sense of self.

There is a belief that this sense of self is here always, but now, we have come to see that this is not true. It just comes and goes, many times a day, whenever I identify with this body/mind, thoughts, emotions, and sensations. The default human condition is free. This natural holiday, when you are not identifying, happens to everyone. However, it does not have the power to liberate because there is no knowing when it happens.

Know what is true, and this knowing is what sets you free. When a holiday happens, know—I am here, now, aware and free, unborn. That is my nature, who I am.

❦

TIME OUT

The rest of this book is built upon the first inquiry. Although you may be inclined to just continue now, it is extremely important to go back to Inquiry One and go through all of the experiments again, even if you are fairly certain that you "got" them. The second time through, your recognition will be even more certain. Resist the temptation to just continue plowing through. There is no rush. The full recognition of all of these experiments is essential for coming to the end of seeking forever.

INQUIRY TWO — VALUING WHAT IS TRUE

Once there is a shift of knowing, the key to liberating this mind is valuing what is true. But you can't value something until you have come to know its value. So, let's find out what value this recognition has.

Ordinary — Not Special

We have been taught our whole life to value the ever-changing aspect of who we are—thoughts, ideas, beliefs, body, experiences, circumstances, relationships, money, etc. These things do have value in a relative sense, but we have come to value these things to a perverse degree. That is why this world is such a mess—because we value self above everything. We have come to value that which is in constant change, flux, and decay, so we feel insecure.

Valuing self makes us feel very special, the special me. Being special creates suffering for yourself and others. That's why most seekers don't want to come to know truth, because they don't want to give up being special—my special experiences,

97

my special connection with god, my special enlightenment, etc.

Let's see something different. Have a holiday and see. Have we attained any new kind of elevated consciousness? It is just ordinary, isn't it? The natural human condition is free. That doesn't make us special, does it? It's true for everyone whether they know it or not. See for yourself.

When we come to know liberation, we are very happy to be ordinary. Needing to be special is suffering. It is a relief to no longer need to be special.

I would say it is valuable to know this.

Mental Health

What we have been doing in the psychological model is trying to come to mental health or clarity. It is the same in the spiritual model. We try to arrange things in the mind so that we feel there is stability and order. We try to purify our minds for this reason. If you refer to this body/mind in this way and see that there is always something going on with it, you will say, "I am not healthy."

But, here and now, notice something. Have a holiday and see that there is stability, clarity, and health already. If you know what is true, how can you deny that your essential being is health itself—free, unbound, pure and clear. Have a look.

For most people, the psychological and spiritual models may have some benefit. For someone who wants to be free and is ready to jump off the carousel of mind, they see that their essential being is already health. The natural human condition is health.

I would say it is valuable to know this.

No Sense of Lack — Complete and Whole

When you came out of the womb, was there any sense of lack or incompleteness? That is something we start to believe when we take a birth of self. When we start to believe that the amalgamation of impressions in our brain is who we are, we come to believe that there is something wrong with us. I am lacking something—I need more love, wealth, acclaim, etc. Then we realize that none of that ultimately fulfills us and we are still lacking, so we get on the spiritual path and do the same thing. Now, we are lacking enlightenment— Buddha is so great, and we are not. We seek spiritual experiences, understanding, and purity. All of this is becoming, and it all stems from a sense of lack, that there is something inherently not complete about me.

Would we seek anything if we knew we lacked nothing and in fact were complete already?

Have a holiday now and see. Are you lacking anything? Are you not complete already? Don't refer to the beliefs in your mind, instead recognize your essential being.

❦

Do you need god, enlightenment, a relationship, or more money to be complete? Who would need these things? Clearly, it's the personal self, right? Don't refer to this body/mind, instead recognize your essential being. Here and now, I am complete and whole. Look for yourself and see this.

❦

If it's true that you are complete and lack nothing, then what more is there to seek?

I would say it is valuable to know this.

Intelligence — Life Itself

What we traditionally value as intelligence is one's IQ level. But clearly, there are many people with high IQ's that exhibit little wisdom. And having a high IQ certainly does not guarantee happiness or peace of mind.

So then, what is true intelligence, the intelligence that brings wisdom and peace of mind? When you recognize your essential being, you recognize that it is aware, that this aware is knowing, and this knowing is intelligence itself. It is the intelligence of life itself. See this yourself.

True intelligence is your essential being, who I am. In this intelligence, there is wisdom. Have a look, now and see.

We believe that we are in life or that we have life. But have a look and see, isn't it true that who I am is life itself?

This, which is aware, is intelligently aware. This is the true intelligence, life itself, who you are. Another name for you is intelligence, life itself.

I would say it is valuable to know this.

Comparison

We compare ourselves with others and suffer because of it. This person has more money than I do, or this person is more successful, better looking, etc. So, we feel inferior and that we are lacking something. Or, conversely, we feel superior to others because we have more money, success, a bigger house, or whatever. Seekers compare too. For example, "Ramana Maharshi is more enlightened than I am," or "The Buddha is enlightened, and I am not." So, we feel inferior. But we feel superior to the right-wing, Evangelical Christian because they are obviously lost and asleep.

What are we comparing? We are comparing our sense or idea of self with the idea of self of another. My ego vs. your ego. This comparing of self/ego causes a lot of personal suffering and suffering in this world as well. Comparison is the root of conflict and war—interpersonal, international, interreligious, etc. "My religion is better than yours." "You have more land than I have, and I want it." "I don't have enough oil, so I will take it from you." "We are having a disagreement in our relationship and I need to be right, I need to win." Comparison is the creation and result of the belief in a separate self—the belief in ego as the center of the universe.

Not only do we compare ourselves with others, we even, and almost more insidiously, compare ourselves to ourselves. We compare who we are now to an ideal of who we think we need to become, always in the future. Now, we are not pure enough, or fulfilled enough, or wealthy enough, or enlightened enough. We go on to the next teaching, the next teacher, the next Satsang, always hoping we will find this fulfillment of our ideas and concepts about what we need to become.

Again, we are comparing this self/ego, but this time with the new and improved self/ego that we will be in the future. So, we keep seeking and striving in the hope that at some point in the future we will arrive at this ideal picture of ourselves and then we will be complete. While, in the meantime, we feel we are inadequate, lacking, or inferior. But that time never comes, the ideal is never realized. We keep seeking because we feel there is something wrong with us, that we are lacking something, that we are not yet "there."

When we value self—meaning our beliefs about who we are and our beliefs about the world—above our essential being, then we are in a perverse relationship with ourselves and everything around us. This can stop.

When we come to know our essential being, we see that we are whole and complete already, that we lack nothing, that we are free, and that we don't need to have our beliefs and opinions validated. When we come to know our essential being, we realize that it is true for everyone, whether they know it or not. So, why would we feel superior or inferior? When we know our essential being is complete, why would there be greed or envy, the causes of so much suffering?

Instead of valuing these ever-changing impressions, these limited views of yourself and the world, value your essential being. Value it above all else. See the freedom in who you are— free from the need to compare, free from the need to be inferior, superior, or even equal, and free to be happily who you are now, a completely unique expression of the one whole that is your essential being, and the essential being of everyone.

Who you are right now has to be true. Why? Because it is who you are right now, and there is only now. Any ideas you have about who you should be in the future have to be false. Why? Because they are imagination, fantasy, lies. If, now, you are appearing as joy, then that is true because it is actual, now. If, now, you are appearing as anger, then that is true because it is actual, now. The appearances change constantly, never to return in the same way again. But you, your essential being (aware, free, pure, complete, and whole, here and now) doesn't change. Value this and be finished with comparison. Have a holiday and see what is true. See now.

I would say it is valuable to know this.

Space for You to Be

One of the truly authentic teachers I met was Douglas Harding. He has one of the most beautiful sayings and it has huge implications. He said, "Can't you see, I'm just space for you to be." Let's have a look and see what he means.

The normal way that we are in this world is: "Can't you see, I'm just a psychological mess for you to deal with." or "Can't you see, I'm just a bundle of beliefs for you to agree with, and if you don't agree, you are wrong." Isn't that why the world is as it is?

However, "Can't you see, I'm just space for you to be." Isn't this a far better way to show up in the world? In truth, this is who you are. See this for yourself.

I would say it is valuable to know this.

Free Already

Have a look, now. You are free already. Haven't you always been free, even though you didn't know it? Look now, without referring to mind, past or future. Is there any reason to seek further for freedom? Isn't seeking already finished, now? Of course, if you go back into your mind, with all of its concepts and doubts, you will think you are missing something and that there is more to attain or understand. But, if you don't do that, and you recognize your essential being of freedom, now, then you can see that, here and now, it is already finished. If you don't go looking in your mind, you will see that, here and now, it is already doubtless.

I would say it is valuable to know this.

Value Review

Let us review the value of what we have recognized.

- I have been here my whole life, I haven't changed at all.
- I am and always have been free.
- I am ordinary; I no longer need to be special. It is a burden to need to be special and a relief not to have to be. This is true health, mental and emotional health, and clarity.
- I am here, now, always
- My essential being is true intelligence, life itself.
- I lack nothing, here and now, I am complete. I don't need more enlightenment. I don't need to seek anything other than what I am. I don't need to envy or to covet. I don't need to feel inferior or superior.
- I am just space for others to be, not a psychological mess to present to the world.

There is a lot of value in knowing these things. Now that we know this, it is possible to value it. This is the true value that provides health and freedom. If you value this more than anything, then this mind will be liberated. Know what is true and truth will set you free. Why? Because you are already free.

Liberation is simply the end of seeking. Once you know that you are complete and lack nothing, seeking is finished.

When holidays happen, know the value. If something appears, like greed, jealousy, or whatever, no problem. No need to judge. Just know that it is coming from identification with self, a sense of lack. Don't do anything about it; just know again that you lack nothing.

The Value of Freedom

Without any judgment, let's see how we are operating. If a story appears in the mind and you notice that you are getting involved in it, looping around and trying to resolve it and going over it again and again, which is suffering, then, obviously, this is what you want in that moment. You do not want freedom, because if you do, it is here, now, already. This is not bad, or a judgment, it is just seeing what is true, that the story is what you want in this moment.

In the midst of that, you may have a holiday. When you do, get real. Know that there is no resolution in your mind and stay on holiday. Those stories are not real. What is real is here and now, freedom.

If you go into those mental loops, you might stay on the same loop for the rest of your life. Clearly, that is what you want. No problem. But, if you want freedom, it is here.

We are beginning to recognize much more about our essential being. See for yourself if the following is true about who you are.

You are:

Aware — Have a holiday and see if this is true.

All-Inclusive — Have a holiday and see if this is true.

Free — Have a holiday and see if this is true.

Now — Have a holiday and see if this is true.

No self — Have a holiday and see if this is true.

Unborn — Have a holiday and see if this is true.

Pure — Have a holiday and see if this is true.

Ordinary — Have a holiday and see if this is true.

Intelligence — Have a holiday and see if this is true.

Life Itself — Have a holiday and see if this is true.

Lacking Nothing — Have a holiday and see if this is true.

Whole and Complete — Have a holiday and see if this is true.

Free Already — Have a holiday and see if this is true.

Again, as you can see, none of these can be objectified, as in a thing that you are, they are simply what is true about your essential being.

Please make sure you see the value of everything pointed to above. Read through it again, have holidays, and see. When it is clear, move on.

INQUIRY TWO: QUESTIONS AND ANSWERS

Relationships

Inquirer: Some days, I have a crisis. I am single, and I would like to have a partner. It's very tiring, and I suffer. I can't see that it's not me. I just see these thoughts in my mind.

Sal: Do you think you need to get rid of those thoughts?

Inquirer: In that moment, I feel desperation and I can't see anything else other than that. I remember your words, "It's fine if that happens, it's fine because you are aware, so when you next have a holiday, you will see that you are aware." So, I calm down and then, later in the afternoon, I have a holiday and it's easy, but in the moment of a crisis it's impossible.

Sal: Let's have a holiday, now.

Sal: You know what's true. Here and now, I'm free. In fact, it's always been this way, you just didn't notice.

Inquirer: Yes.

Sal: Are you lacking anything?

Inquirer: No.

Sal: Are you incomplete in any way? Or are you already complete?

Inquirer: I am complete.

Sal: Let me ask you. The thought, "I need to have a partner, a relationship." Aren't they there because there is a sense of lack, of not being complete? Because I am not complete without a partner, without a relationship, I am lacking.

Inquirer: Yes

Sal: Let's have another holiday.

❧

Sal: Is that true or not?

Inquirer: No.

Sal: When you came out of the womb, did you think, "I need to have a partner?"

Inquirer: *No.*

Sal: That's very interesting. "I am incomplete because I don't have a partner."

Inquirer: *(laughs) No.*

Sal: It's not a problem, we're not changing anything, we just see why this is occurring. It's programmed in this mind by our culture that you're not complete without a partner in your life.

It's perfectly fine that those feelings and thoughts arise for you, no problem. Just continue to know that you are already complete. You don't need the other to be complete. You are not lacking that either.

Inquirer: *Yes, I know, but in the moment of a crisis it's very suffocating.*

Sal: I understand. If this crisis comes, then it comes, it's an experience, right?

Inquirer: *Yes.*

Sal: What happens with every experience that comes?

Inquirer: *It comes and goes.*

Sal: Yes. Who remains through all of it?

Inquirer: *Me. The real me, the true me.*

Sal: Know that these thoughts and feelings are completely natural because they are just impressions in your mind and they are just playing out. That's the mind's job. They will just play out, there's nothing you can do about it. You don't have to argue with it when it's there: "Oh no, I can't have a holiday, I am so unenlightened now."

This feeling that you need a boyfriend appears, then what do you do? You think, "Oh my god, this is stupid, why am I thinking this, I've got to stop thinking this, I need to have a holiday." Arguing with what is just makes it worse. It's perfectly natural for these feelings and thoughts to appear, and it's perfectly natural for them to go as well.

Here, we have an ocean, life, this is who I am, ocean. Then a wave appears, "I need a partner." In the moment that wave is appearing, isn't it still ocean?

Inquirer: *Yes.*

Sal: It's still ocean, not some separate wave, it's ocean. So, when ocean is appearing as wave, who are you in that moment? You're that feeling and that sensation, "I need a partner." That's who you are appearing as, in that moment. Now, I am appearing as peace and stillness, and now, I am appearing as the wave, "I need a partner."

All of these changes come and go. The wave appears and then the thoughts come, "Oh no, I am doing badly, I am being a bad student. Oh my god, I am not getting enlightened and I'll never be enlightened. I need to have a holiday." And, before you know it, you have a tidal wave, a tsunami.

What happens if you just let that wave come, and then go. There's no more judging yourself that you're doing badly. Did you create that wave?

Inquirer: No, it just appeared.

Sal: Right, if you didn't create it then you can't make it go away either. This wave was just impressed in your brain by culture. You didn't create it, did you? When you came out of the womb, you didn't have it, did you?

Inquirer: No.

Sal: When you came out of the womb, did you say, "I will start creating some waves now, I will create something called a partner, I am going to invent it, I am inventing something called a relationship, and then I am going to suffer because of it." No, this just happened in culture, right? Your brain recorded this information, you didn't create it. And, if you didn't create it, then you had nothing to do with it. In this way, what comes, comes, and what goes, goes.

Enlightened or not, there will be trouble and thoughts. For me too, things can happen, circumstances arise with a loved one, and it doesn't feel good. Thoughts can come, unpleasant emotional experiences can come, for anyone, enlightened or not, but I don't argue with it. I am not arguing and thinking, "I am so unenlightened now, oh my god," which leads to the wave getting bigger. And then thinking, "Oh my god, I've got to go back into meditation again, and I need another spiritual teacher."

Don't expect those thoughts to go away. Give yourself a break. If they are there, no problem. It's fine. More importantly, have a holiday and really know what's true, once and for all—you lack nothing, you are complete. Value that!

Anxiety

> *Inquirer: Anxiety arises that I am not going to get the result I am after, like at work for example.*

Sal: Hindu philosophy has what is called Karma Yoga. It is not the Karma that is commonly understood. It means that you are entitled to desire whatever you desire. Why? Because you don't create those desires, they are just appearing. What you are not entitled to is to decide the outcome. Thinking you are in control of the outcome causes this anxiety. If this is fully reconciled in your mind, it is liberation.

> *Inquirer: We are conditioned to think that if we meet our goals, we will be whole and complete, etc.*

Sal: Yes, so let's have a holiday, now.

❧

Sal: Are you lacking anything?

> *Inquirer: No.*

Sal: Are you whole and complete already?

> *Inquirer: Yes.*

Sal: Then, I say, "Get real." Stop messing around.

Inquirer: In the solar plexus, where angst appears for me...

Sal: Then you are not getting real. You have a holiday and then two seconds later, you are back in the solar plexus.

Inquirer: Yes, right.

Sal: Then, what are you doing?

Inquirer: Copping out.

Sal: It is a tendency, no problem. It is what we are taught to do, to overly value the feelings in this body. This body doesn't feel good, so I am not doing well. There is some angst, etc. I say ignore that. Get real, see again that you lack nothing.

Where do you want to live, freedom and truth, or this mental nuthouse? This form is always going to have something going on. These anxieties dissipate when you don't overly value them anymore. There is no inherent power in them. The "on" switch to this suffering is belief. I say, "Have a holiday." If you say, "I am lacking nothing," and a second later, you believe this anxiety means something. You are not getting real.

Inquirer: *I get that.*

Sal: Good. That is why I say value what is true and stop valuing what you have been taught to value, which is these ideas you have learned, like, there is anxiety and I need to get rid of it. If anxiety is there, maybe there is a cause that can be resolved by some action on your part. Then do that. But to try to remove the anxiety itself is futile. If it is appearing, then that is what is.

Trying to get rid of anxiety by pushing it away or trying to understand the psychological foundation for it (which is again the carousel of mind), just supports it and creates a bigger wave.

Inquirer: *The tendency is for the mind to believe it is real.*

Sal: The tendency is for you to believe it is real. Forget this mind. Mind isn't your enemy that is causing you problems. There is only you, and if you believe, then you believe. You are referring to thoughts. It is something that is just appearing, and you buy into them. When you came out of the womb, you didn't buy into anything. Eventually, after they pounded it into your head for a few months, you bought into the idea that you were separate, original sin. Then you said, "Ok, I surrender, I am separate, you win." You have been losing ever since.

I say get real. Stop trying to figure all this stuff out. That is just placing value on the content of this brain. It is simple, isn't it? Just give up, get real.

You recognize truth and then, one second later, there is some anxiety and the belief switch gets turned back on. It's true for everyone, not just you. There's no problem here. My job is just to tell you to get real, now. This is why I say it takes a great maturity to recognize, but a far greater maturity to be finished. Because you jump off of this stuff, and you stay jumped. Not that you are doing jumping, there is no doer. It just happens, when you are ready.

Inquirer: *I understand, the deeper maturity is just letting go totally.*

Sal: There's no letting go, that just happens. The deeper maturity is to just be finished. It happens when it happens. I don't subscribe to the letting go theory, there is no one to let go of anything. You are just creating another self who is letting go. So, I don't say to let go of anything.

The true mature person is just finished. It is just getting real. But see that it's not something you are doing. I say, "Get real." Now, that seed is in your head, and it happens by itself. It happens because you get fed up trying to figure all this stuff out. You are very intelligent, you have read far too much, just like I did, and so it just takes some time to resolve these doubts.

I have no argument with what is. Good or bad, I don't argue; it is what it is. I am not trying to become something other than what this very moment is presenting—I am not trying to escape it, or transcend it to a better place, or avoid it, etc. I am just finished with all of that. If there is a kidney stone attack, it hurts like crazy and I roll around like anyone else and take pain killers. If someone I love is suffering, I feel pain. That's life. This body is not supposed to feel good all the time.

Just being finished, ordinary you, that's it. It's the booby prize, seemingly, but, in truth, it is the ultimate prize. It is the booby prize because we think enlightenment is going to give us transcendence, but it is simply not true. The booby prize is the grand prize. You are who you are. Whatever is appearing is appearing, no problem. It's just a wave not separate from ocean. Now, self is appearing as anxiety, it is just a wave, then it goes, and the natural default condition is free, always, even in the midst of the wave, you are free.

What is the Value of a Holiday?

We attend almost exclusively to the impressions in our mind, to our body, to sensations, and to feelings. We believe these things are essentially who we are. When you have a holiday and stop attending to those things, you see something different. You see that you are free and whole, lacking nothing.

If you put your attention on so-called negative thoughts, then you feel pain because of it. You believe thoughts mean something. That's why it's good (right in the middle of these thoughts, whenever it naturally happens) to have a holiday and see something different—in truth, you don't need anything, you are already complete, lacking nothing, and you are already free and whole. Then, if you go right back in there, "I need a partner," or whatever it may be, no problem. A minute later, an hour later, or a week later, whenever it naturally happens, a holiday comes, "I am free, I am complete, I lack nothing."

A holiday is not to get relief from the thoughts and feelings. Yes, you can get a little relief for a moment, but that's not the point. The point is to see what's true. Know what's true, and truth will set you free. It is the recognition of truth that resolves these misidentifications. It is not to experience a little bit of relief and the experience will set you free. You have a holiday and you know what's true. Now, I know—I lack nothing, it's finished.

INQUIRY THREE — TIME

Time

When you have a holiday, you recognize that all there is, is now. Without going into your mind, the only thing you can know, and confirm for yourself, is what is, here and now. Have a look and see that this is true. If you do not use thoughts about the past, then it is very clear that in reality all there is, is now. This is simply true, see this.

❧

If it is true that there is only now, then, did anything ever happen? If you go into the mind, and say, "I remember something from the past," then you are not doing what is suggested here. You are on the carousel of mind. Without using thoughts at all, without using memory, just here and now only, is there any reality to past? Look and see.

❧

I am saying, "Get real." There is only this, here and now. Past and future are fantasy.

Freedom is only now. Freedom is not in the mind of past and future. It is not in thought, memory, fantasy, or hope. It is only here, now. Past and future are the carousel of mind. If you want freedom, it is here, now. It will not happen in some imaginary future.

To be truthful, THERE IS NO TIME. And if there is no time, then in truth, NOTHING EVER HAPPENED.

You will say, "But yesterday I did this or that." But again, do not refer to your thoughts; where is that, NOW?

If you get real and jump off of this mind, simply here and now, then the only truth that you can confirm is what is. The only thing you can know is now. Everything that is not now is not real. In that case, see, nothing ever happened.

~⚬≈~

Just like there's no past, there's no future either. If there is no future, what is there to become? Future is only a projection of the mind. In truth, there is no future, and so there is no becoming. There is no truth to ideas like, "I will be free in the future." or "I will be better in the future." or "I am going to die in the future." Why? Because there is no future, there's only now.

~⚬≈~

The point of this recognition is to be finished with the psychological suffering associated with past (personal history), and future (seeking and becoming). We assign blame to ourselves as well as to others like our parents, things like regret, remorse and guilt—these emotions are based on events that, right now, are only thoughts or memories of the past. But those events are not real, now. They are fantasy. Look now, where are they? THEY ARE NOT! They have no truth and no existence at all. And, if they are not, there is no point in giving them any value at all. That is, if you want freedom.

When you hold on to these things, you are a victim. You are a victim of a phantom because the past and future are not real. If you are mature, you will jump off that carousel. By jumping, you give up the victimization of psychology, past and future. These stories are a lie, aren't they? Why? Because there is no past or future, and since there is no past or future, then every story you ever told yourself is simply a fantasy, now. If you want truth, then you will not accept these fantasies.

Jump off of that carousel. Give up the right to be a victim of psychology—your past and future.

❧

What is, is, now. Knowing this and being reconciled with this is liberation from seeking and becoming, liberation from victimization, and liberation from past and future. This is really jumping off the carousel. Have a holiday now and see this.

❧

Time as a Practical Device

Time is a mental creation. It is a necessary concept to be used practically for navigating life. If, tomorrow, I need to book a bus ticket to NY, then I put that on my calendar. We use time to function in this world of appearance, the Play of Life. As a practical consideration, it is useful. But, and this is important, using time as a means of analyzing yourself because of the past or because of something you are going to become in the future, is fantasy and causes suffering. Freedom will never be found in either.

Knowing truth is freedom from past suffering and freedom from future becoming. Do you see what I am saying?

Being Here, Now

Be here now is a technique to, temporarily, bring you out of the thinking process. It's a good practice for someone on the path. But we're coming to know something different. There's only now, right? Is there any other possibility than to be now? Can you not be here, now? Have a holiday, now and see for yourself.

You can't. You don't have to try to be here, now, because you have no choice. If you're "lost" in thoughts of the past, you're still being here, now.

People love to dwell on the past. People are in their stories about what happened to them, the poor me and great me stories, their whole life. So then, the teaching says, be here now, so you can stop that for a moment. That's not what I am saying.

What we're doing is coming to reckon finally that there's only now, that's it. Then you lose interest in those fantasies, because you want truth. I don't dwell on the past. Those sentimental or painful thoughts rarely even happen here because I know they are a fantasy. I find all that stuff boring, thinking about the so-called past.

Know what's true and truth will set you free. There is only now, that's it, there's no other choice. There's nothing behind the curtain. This is it. There's only now. When this is reckoned with, you stop buying into the stories because it's just known that it is illusion. So, you don't have to drag yourself into the now every five minutes, because it's finished. You simply lose interest in the stories.

You Have no History

Let's have a look, now. Have a holiday. Here and now, you are free, right?

***

Freedom is who you are, and if freedom has no history, then you have no history. I am not even a thing; how can no thing have a history? There's now, my essential, free nature, and everything is just passing through—body, thoughts, experiences—but I have no history, I am free.

***

That's why freedom isn't for many people, because who is willing to give up their history?

Stories

Past stories are the history of self. These stories mean nothing because they are not actual, now. Whatever appears to have happened in the past, only appears now, in your memory; it has no actuality, now. It is by weaving these incidents into stories and believing they mean something that they are empowered and cause pain and suffering in this moment. We bind our concept of our self to the stories, thus creating bondage. The incidents no longer exist, and the stories are created, now, in your mind. The stories are not real.

This message is not for everyone. It's for a very mature person who wants freedom, real freedom, truth. It's a huge relief. It's a burden to continue dwelling on stories, it is bondage.

Self Needs Time to Exist

When you take a birth of self, what's born is time. Because, when I take a birth of self, I have a history. But, if there is no self, there is no history. The birth of self is the birth of time. Self cannot exist without time. Self is synonymous with time. Without past or future there is no story of self. Self needs time to exist. In no time, there is no self. Have a holiday, now and see this, in no time.

There's no time—past, history, becoming. There is just now. Look, now. Where is the "self?"

Yes, there are sensations in the body, but that doesn't mean there is a self. It is just a sensation appearing in who I am, aware. Look and see.

❦

Another name for you is now. Again, not an object. Have a holiday. I am, now?

❦

Aware, all-inclusive, free, life, unborn, here and now.
Is it true? Don't believe what you read. See if it is true.

❦

World is an Illusion

You've heard that this world is an illusion—the world is not real, objects are not real, they're an illusion. What does that mean? The way I say it is that our senses perceive at a particular, gross, level. For example, the eyes perceive at a particular level that the brain puts together as forms. If you looked at a coffee cup through a very high-powered microscope, what would you see? You would see space. There would be space with some quarks floating around.

In truth, at our gross level of perception (tactile, auditory, and visual), form appears solid. But, if we had high power microscopic eyeballs, we would see that this is nothing but space, just space with some atoms floating around. So, in truth, this is not solid.

The line on the edge of a cup, which looks very obvious to you, does not exist under a high-powered microscope. There is no line; it's just space with atoms floating around. Use your imagination, and you'll see. This cup is not an object that is separated from air. Only at our gross level of perception do we create solidity like this. This is necessary because that's how we are able to function in the realm of form.

Look at your body, the line of your arm. At a microscopic level, there's no line, is there? That's the truth. However, we just see it with our gross level senses. Your arm is not separate from air, it's space with little tiny atoms. Essentially what is, is space.

The ancient sages said, "Form is an illusion." Yes, it's an illusion, in the sense that it is not solid. It's only solid to our gross level perceptions. Our perceptions are not ultimately true or accurate. But I do not write form off as simply illusion because, at the level of our human perception, it appears solid and this is our experience. It is how this human form functions.

We believe we're going to come to a place of enlightenment where we're going to see that everything is an illusion, and it will be some kind of new state of consciousness.

But our senses do function at this gross level, that's what's happening. So, to go to the extreme of saying form is an illusion is pointless. We come full circle and we fully accept form because that's how we perceive. We don't deny, and we don't say, "Form is an illusion and I am awareness, so I don't have to take care of this body/mind organism."

∽⚬⚬∾

Eternal Life

Some teachings say that after you die, you're going to have eternal life—it's going to be forever. Somehow, you are going to live forever. Let's have a holiday, now.

∽⚬⚬∾

There's only now, right? Throughout your entire life, through all experiences, you have been here, now, and free, even though you didn't notice. Ten years ago, twenty years ago, it's been now all along. It's always now, no matter when you look. When you're ninety, it's going to be now.

Eternal life has nothing to do with time. It is eternally now. Who I am is life. I am not going to attain eternal life, forever. I am life eternal. This is who I am. No matter when I look, when I came out of the womb until the day I die, it's always now.

Within me, who I am now, forms are changing. Waves are coming and going, including the wave of this body and these thoughts and sensations. Within me, aware, this body is growing and disintegrating. Thoughts and sensations are coming and going within who I am, now.

Your essential aware nature never changes, does it? Forms never stay the same, do they? Things come, things go. Businesses come, businesses go. Young body comes, young body goes. Yet, I remain the same. If I know that things come and go and that's just the way it is, then I can relax when things go. It's just the way it is. Our fears about losing things and our concerns about things changing are not useful because everything changes, that's just true.

The fear of change is programmed into our mind and it is not beneficial. If we want truth, then truth is true—everything changes, everything comes, and everything goes. Being reconciled with that is the peace that passes understanding. Know that you will gain and lose many more things in this life. Okay, that's what is.

There's no Place Like Home

Here is my take on The Wizard of Oz. It is a story about a journey on the spiritual path and finally coming full circle.

Dorothy lives in Kansas. She is disillusioned, people are mean and cruel, and she feels that something is lacking in her life. So, she runs away from home, the prodigal daughter, seeking fulfillment and love. On the road, she meets a gypsy wizard who has a crystal ball, a wealth of exotic knowledge, and many fantastical stories. She gets excited hearing about the possibility of something that transcends her mundane, ordinary life. This was Dorothy's introduction to spiritual seeking.

A huge cyclone starts brewing and she runs towards the safety of the only home she knows. This storm represents a turning point in her life, one that shifts her mind and puts her squarely on the spiritual path. When she arrives back to her house, instead of finding safety, she is knocked unconscious because of the storm. And, when she wakes up, everything is different. She is now in a full-color world, filled with new people, new landscapes, exciting new possibilities, and adventures—the spiritual path.

She meets her first guide, Glinda, the Good Witch of the North. She tells Glinda that she wants to go home and asks her for help. Glinda says that if she wants to go home, she will have to go and meet the Great Wizard, because he is all-knowing, all-powerful and he alone can help her.

> Dorothy: "...I'd give anything to get out of Oz altogether, but which is the way back to Kansas? I can't go the way I came."

> Glinda: "No, that's true. The only person who might know would be the great and wonderful Wizard of Oz himself."

So, Dorothy begins walking on the Yellow Brick Road to meet the Wizard. Along the way, she encounters the three paths of Advaita Vedanta. First, she meets the Scarecrow, who represents Jnana. Jnana is the path of self-inquiry. The

Scarecrow wants a brain, he wants to know. Then she meets the Tin Man, who represents Bhakti, or devotion. He wants a heart, to have true love. Then she meets the Cowardly Lion, who represents Karma. In Vedanta, Karma means that you're entitled to want what you want but you're not entitled to choose the outcome of your actions. It is the courage to live life now, as it is, without knowing or having any control over what will happen. The Lion wants the courage to live like this.

Dorothy and her friends are on the spiritual path, a path to fulfillment, to coming home. On the way, they are confronted by many obstacles, including the Wicked Witch of the West and her Flying Monkeys. These represent ego and mental habits (vasanas, the apparent, conceptual blocks to awakening). To proceed, they have to avoid and get past these obstacles.

As they are approaching Emerald City, where the Great Wizard lives, they take a detour, (which they believe is a shortcut), through a field of poppies, and begin having a profound and deep spiritual experience. This experience is immensely blissful and very compelling, and they begin to fall asleep, potentially, and dangerously, getting stuck there. This is what we as seekers do, we believe that spiritual or mystical experiences, because of their extraordinary insightfulness and/or heightened sensory experience, are the thing we are seeking, and so, we get stuck, never inquiring beyond them. But, the Scarecrow, having a wise insight, realizes that they cannot stay there, this is not the goal, and they need to keep moving.

Finally, they arrive at the big ashram and meet the Big Guru, the Wizard of Oz. He is behind a curtain, projecting a giant image—one of omnipotence, omniscience and intimidation. In their own sense of unworthiness, they feel lowly and pathetic in comparison, just as most seekers do when they meet the Big Guru.

> *Wizard: "I am Oz, the Great and Powerful. Who are you?"*

> *Dorothy: "I am Dorothy, the small and meek ..."*

Dorothy, trembling with fear and reverence, timidly tells him that she wants to go home. He proclaims in his booming voice that he can help. But first, she will have to do one thing—she will have to kill the evil ego.

> *Dorothy: "What must I do?"*

> *Wizard: "...you must prove yourself worthy by performing a very small task. Bring me the broomstick of the Wicked Witch of the West."*

With great fear and anticipation, they go out and seek the Wicked Witch. They are convinced that the task will be extremely difficult and dangerous, in fact, almost impossible. First, they have to get past the Flying Monkeys and the soldiers, whom are rife with danger. But finally, finding and confronting the Wicked Witch, Dorothy accidentally throws a little water on her face, and miraculously, the Witch melts into nothing, exposing her true powerlessness and essential emptiness.

With the Witch's broomstick in hand, they go back to the guru to report their adventure. Dorothy's dog, Toto, who represents discrimination, notices something and pulls the curtain away, exposing the Wizard for who he is—just a regular little guy, not an all-knowing being. Still trying to fool them, he booms,

> *"Pay no attention to that man behind the curtain.*
> *The Great and Powerful Oz has spoken!"*

But it is too late, he is exposed, and they see that he is just a regular, ordinary man, fully human. It was just his grand show of powers, complicit with their own sense of unworthiness, that created their belief of him being special and far greater than them.

> *Dorothy: "...You're a very bad man!"*

*Wizard: "Oh, no, my dear I'm a very good man.
I'm just a very bad wizard."*

Dorothy is devastated, she has tried everything, all to no avail. She is completely frustrated, he can't help her, and she is at the end of the line. Now, she is ready to hear the simple truth.

At that moment, Glinda, the Good Witch of the North, reappears.

Dorothy: "Oh, will you help me? Can you help me?"

Glinda: "You don't need to be helped any longer. You've always had the power to go back to Kansas."

Dorothy: "I have?"

Scarecrow: "Then why didn't you tell her before?"

Glinda: "Because she wouldn't have believed me. She had to learn it for herself."

The Tin Man asks Dorothy what she has learned. She says that the next time she wants to find happiness, she will know that it is not somewhere "out there," but here only, within her own heart. Dorothy had tried everything. She went on the seeking path, had all the spiritual experiences, and met the Big Guru. She tried it all and finding that the answer was not in any of those external objects, she was ready to simply "look within" and be a "light unto herself."

After clicking her heels together and saying, "There's no place like home," she awakens in her own bedroom in Kansas. Around her are her Aunt and Uncle, her friends, and all the ordinary, everyday things of her life. But now, Dorothy sees them all in a new light. The Land of Oz was half circle, it was just another part of the appearance (the Maya). Now, she has come full circle and realizes that this ordinary life, who she has always been, is the transcendence she had sought.

She's had a shift of knowing. Now, there's appreciation and freedom. Relief and deep gratitude well up in her as she sees that she is complete and whole, and always has been. There was no need to change, transcend or make herself into something other than what she is.

"Home! ... I'm not going to leave here ever, ever again ... there's no place like home!"

Coming Full Circle

We're coming full circle. We are not just aware, or as they say, "awareness." We are also the objects that appear. The true meaning of non-dual is the absolute and form are not separate. There is the ocean, perfectly still, eternal, and unmoving—no movement. (This is a metaphor and as such is imperfect.) We can say ocean is the absolute. Then on the surface of the ocean some energy happens, and a wave appears. This wave is whatever is appearing, now. During the course of its appearance, is wave separate from ocean? It's always ocean, isn't it? It's ocean as absolute and ocean as form.

When that wave is appearing, it is always ocean. Wave appears and then vanishes. But, where did it come from? It's just here, now, ocean. Then it is gone, never to be seen again.

Absolute (aware), and form (the appearance) are not separate. We think non-duality means there's no two—me and you. But the true non-duality means absolute and form are not separate.

There are many sayings in history to support this:

Buddhism says, "Form is emptiness, emptiness is form." It doesn't say, "There's emptiness and there's form." It says, "Form is emptiness..."

Buddhism also says, "Samsara is Nirvana." Nirvana is the absolute, and Samsara is the realm of form and suffering.

Hindu philosophy says, "Shiva and Shakti are one." Shiva is the unmanifest, and Shakti is the manifest energy. They say they are one.

Jesus said, "I and my Father are one." I, this form, and my Father, the Absolute, are one. Jesus is trying to tell us the same thing. According to that statement, he was a non-dualist.

The absolute and form are not two—form is the absolute.

The Neo-Advaitans say, "I am awareness, so form doesn't matter." They are halfway there, and this is not the whole truth.

I don't demonize or deny what is appearing now. We're not trying to kill the self. If in this moment, the sense of self is appearing as however it is appearing, it is fine. Form is the appearance of the absolute. There is no absolute apart from form.

What you see is the absolute. So then, if that is so, what is left to seek or transcend? Have a holiday and see.

❦

A True Story

I have a good illustrative true story about halfway around the circle. A few years ago, a friend of mine in India got a bacterial infection in his foot. (You can get some nasty ones in India.) It started off with a little black spot on his foot. Then it turned green and black and started getting bigger. Eventually, it became elephantized. He thought he was very spiritual, only awareness and not the body, so the body didn't matter. He said, "Ha ha ha, it doesn't matter, it is only the body."

People convinced him to go to the doctor, and the doctor said, "You have to take antibiotics, otherwise we'll have to amputate your foot." He said, "Ha ha ha, it doesn't matter because I am not this body." I wrote to him and said, "Come on man, take the antibiotics." He said: "Ha ha ha..." Then, a couple weeks later, his whole leg was black and elephantized. The doctors said, "We're going to have to cut off your leg." Finally, everyone convinced him to take antibiotics.

A year later, he was walking around with two legs and a tiny little scar on his foot. If he hadn't taken the antibiotics, he would have one leg right now, or be dead. And then, how much "ha ha ha" would he be doing?

This conceptual thinking is unreal. We hear and believe these concepts like, "I am not the body, I am just spirit or awareness," or some nonsense like this. It's not true. I am the body. I am whatever is appearing, that's who I am. We don't have to avoid life. We take care of responsibilities like family, work, money, and things that need to be handled. But, know what's true (you are free), and be finished seeking and becoming.

What is truly valuable is freedom. And by valuing freedom, it does not mean you are denying form, but you are not pathologically valuing it either. Before coming to this work, the most important thing in our mind is "me, me, my, my." We start off with this pathological focus on self, then we go to this pathological focus on awareness, and then we come back home to health, truth, and balance. Everything falls into its right and proper place, by itself. Ease of being, with whatever is appearing, everything's coming and going, but we attend to what needs to be attended to. You don't need to become anything or hold on to stories from the past, you see. There is only now.

Romeo and Juliet

Two actors are on stage playing Romeo and Juliet. Romeo realizes he is an actor, while Juliet has forgotten she is an actress, she is convinced she is Juliet. She fully believes her suffering while Romeo knows it is part of the play. But, if Romeo hasn't come full circle, in the middle of the play, he would say, "Wait, I just realized I am an actor, so I have to get off the stage now." That's what people who believe they are not the body and only awareness think.

But, if he has come full circle, he knows he is an actor, and he stays on the stage and puts on the best performance he possibly can. You are an actor in the Play of Life, and you don't have to deny your character. Just because you know you are an actor doesn't mean you have to go and live in a cave and just be awareness. You can still act in the play, and you will win the Academy Award for your character because no one can play you as well as you can.

INQUIRY THREE: QUESTIONS AND ANSWERS

Illusion of a Past

> **Inquirer:** *Our physical appearances seem to point to a past.*

Sal: Mental interpretation of appearances point to a past, the appearance itself points to nothing but what is. There is only now. For one who wants to be free, this is true. Freedom has no history. For one who embraces freedom, there is no history. I say, "You have no history."

Very few people are willing to be reconciled with having no history. People want their past, their story of self. The end of time is the end of the story of me. Being fully reconciled that there is only now is liberation. This is stark, but we are getting real here. The purpose of this is not philosophical, it is the end of seeking, the end of becoming.

As an ego/self, you are only stories. So, when the stories go, you (the ego/self) go. Freedom from past and future is freedom from self. The end of becoming. Becoming in the future has to do with impressions in our mind like, "I have heard there is enlightenment, so how do I attain it in the future?"

> **Inquirer:** *And that brings in fear and anxiety about getting something in the future to assure some security.*

Sal: That's right. But that security is false; you have no idea what is going to happen. The only true security is now because that doesn't change. Now, not knowing anything about past and future, and not needing to know, is a relief.

⧼⧽

Nothing Ever Happened? What About Regret?

> **Inquirer:** *I am having a hard time seeing there is no past and nothing ever happened. Yes, I see that "who I am" doesn't have a history, and what happened in the past is just a thought in my mind—now. But, I feel "Amanda" has a history... "Amanda" in the play has a past. This is true, right?*

I know "Amanda" is just an idea I have been taught, and all these impressions have created this character. If there is no self, then there is no Amanda. Ok fine, not real. But that doesn't help for something Amanda said/did a couple of days ago that she regrets! This body/mind... Amanda, the actress playing her role... is affected by something she did in the past.

I am confused. I guess I can say, "I am just appearing as mind regretting the repercussions, now." But what happened is not real, and it never happened, what!? Leave this body and mind behind? I could be like... doesn't matter, who cares, whatever. Is this irresponsible? I am afraid to be like the guy who almost got his leg cut off!

Sal: Yes, the story "Amanda" has a past. But, in truth, there is only now. By valuing the story of Amanda, to what I call a pathological and perverse extreme, which is how we are taught and what we do, we suffer, unnecessarily. If you said or did something a couple days ago that was not so wise, then it is recorded as an impression in your mind, as are all experiences. Then, the mind replays that back as thought; that is its function. Because we are taught to believe that we are the doer, chooser, thinker, creator and actor, we judge ourselves harshly, or conversely, take undo credit for something positive.

It's not quite the same as the guy who almost had his leg cut off. He was ignoring something that was occurring in the present, to potentially great harm to his body. You are regretting something you cannot change because it's not occurring, now. So, there is nothing you can do about it. If I say or do something unwise, I can be reminded of it as well, and a regret can appear. But it is more of a recognition. To hold on to that does nothing but create suffering for you.

This is a very timely question you ask because our next session is about just this—is there a doer, chooser, thinker, creator, or actor? Is there free will? It is a very profound inquiry, you will see.

Be natural, the mind will do what it does, replaying impressions recorded in it. Since we are taught to blame and judge, to moralize and condemn, based on doership, we do so to ourselves and others.

In the realm of appearance, the play, there is the appearance of time. It is not to be denied because it is a practical device used in the play. But, used as a psychological device for blaming, regretting, or reminiscing about the past, or for hoping, becoming, and seeking in the future, time causes a lot of suffering. Have a holiday and see that there is only now.

⌘

Full Circle, Form and the Absolute

Inquirer: *It's difficult to find a balance between form and the absolute, the full circle. For me it's difficult. I think the body is important, but not so important.*

Sal: What makes you think that there is something other than form? That there's something transcendent like heaven, awareness, or something else that transcends form? And that you need to balance the two?

Inquirer: *These ideas come from society and culture, that's why I believe that.*

Sal: Exactly, that's my point. We've read or heard that there's some transcendent place like heaven or some transcendent consciousness. We've read these things, but in truth, what we know is this, form, with its ordinary consciousness.

We have ideas that there's something transcendent, so we think, "Okay, I have to transcend this form and be in Nirvana." But they say, "Samsara is Nirvana." It is not, "there is Samsara and then there is Nirvana." It is "Samsara and Nirvana are one."

What we're doing is coming full circle, so that we stop seeking for something better than, or that transcends, what is. That's all. This whole thing about non-separation between form and absolute is not a philosophical idea that you need to understand. It's not an experience you need to have. The only purpose for me speaking about this is to end seeking for something other than this, because what is, is it.

It's not about balancing them, or getting an experience, or understanding. It's just about putting to rest these ideas that there's something other than this, right here and now. There's only now. If there's only now, then whatever is appearing now, must be true. And, if that is true, why argue with what is?

You don't need to balance anything. Be finished with all of that philosophical and psychological stuff. We're not doing anything special here. We're not coming to any specific state, experience, or anything like that. We're just being finished seeking, that's all. What is, is.

When that's fully reconciled, there's nothing more. That's freedom.

❧

Trying to Understand

Inquirer: I see the subtlety of when I keep referring to tendencies. They're not coming from outside; the concept arises within aware. You said that anything that arises is real when it appears. I can't seem to resolve this.

Anything that appears in aware is apparently real. But the only thing that is inherently real is aware. Everything else is just an appearance. So, what I understand you to say is that when something arises in aware, it is real. But I see it being transitory and fleeting.

I know this is a lot of intellectual crap and that I can throw all this out the window, and I don't have to figure it out. But I seem to be stuck with this.

Sal: So then, why are you trying to figure it out? When a wave appears it is not separate from ocean, is it?

Inquirer: The tendency is to relate to the wave as being real.

Sal: There is still a subtle sense with you of trying to transcend something, this mortal limited form. We all hear that enlightenment is transcendence. But I say have a look, now. Do you know what you are looking at? The absolute. This is it. Everything you see is not separate from the absolute; it is the absolute, appearing.

When ocean looks at wave, it is looking at itself, not something separate from itself. These ideas we have of transcendence, of Nirvana, of something other than this apparent form that we are trying to get out of or escape from, are a fantasy. It is not possible to escape what is. Anger, sadness, whatever is appearing, these are waves of truth.

Inquirer: So, trying to escape is just a neurotic tendency to find security and separateness?

Sal: Yes, but why are we trying to transcend or escape? Because we've heard there is something beyond this, and something better, that offers relief and escape from life as it is. But there is no escape. What is, is.

These normal so-called human sufferings aren't going to disappear. What disappears are all the stories we tell ourselves about becoming something "other," or changing what is, or that there is something better than this moment. That suffering can go.

I strongly suggest you go back through Inquiry Three again. We are coming to the end of seeking forever here, and for that to happen, it is very important to see everything clearly. If you just breeze through without really recognizing, it will have little benefit. Once it is all clear, proceed forward.

INQUIRY FOUR — FREE WILL

Is There a Doer, Chooser, Creator, Thinker and Actor? Is There Free Will?

Please go through this inquiry thoroughly. It is important to see this. It is something that many people cannot recognize easily, although it is very obvious once known.

You have most likely heard the concept, "I am not the doer." I say that's misleading because it's not actually that I am not the doer; more accurately it is that there is no doer.

We are trained by culture to believe that we think, we do, we act, we choose, and we have free will. We just take that for granted. But, with a little investigation, we come to see that it's not like that.

If you are a chooser, then there's got to be a "you" in there doing the choosing. Let's find out about that. I use some very simple analogies and experiments so that you can see for yourself.

Movie Analogy

Let's say you're sitting on your sofa, not doing anything in particular, and all of a sudden, a thought comes, "Maybe I should go to a movie tonight." Did you create that thought? Have a look and see.

Are you creating the thought that comes into your head? Or did it just pop in there? Be clear about this. Take a moment to see this.

What's true is you're just sitting there minding your own business and all of a sudden, a thought appears, "Maybe I should go to a movie." Did you create it, or did it just appear?

Is there a little you in there that says, "I am going to now create a thought," and that thought is going to be, "Maybe I should go to a movie?" You didn't create this, did you?

Maybe you are watching TV and a commercial comes on for a new movie. For some reason that movie looks interesting to you. Did you create the thought that it looked interesting, or did it just seem interesting to you? See for yourself.

⚜

Then the next thought comes, "I want to see that." Did you create that thought or did it just appear? Be clear here.

⚜

Did you even create a thing called a movie in the first place? If there was no such thing as a movie, would you have a thought, "Maybe I should go to a movie?"

⚜

No, how could you? You didn't create the fact that there is a movie, you didn't create the specific movie, and the thought, "Maybe I should go to a movie," just appeared. Is it true or not?

⚜

If you recognize that, then we can move on.

You might say, "OK, I didn't create that thought, but I did choose to go." I say, "Oh really? Did you?" Let's see.

The thought comes, "Maybe I should go to a movie," and then the next thought comes, "No, I don't feel like it." If you don't feel like it, did you create that feeling or is that just the feeling that appeared?

The thought, "I don't feel like it," is just what it is. You didn't create that. If the thought came, "Yes, I feel like it," did you create that? No, it is what is. So, if the thought is, "Yes, I feel like it," you might say, "I chose to go to the movie." Is it true? Did you choose? Take your time to be clear about this.

⁜

If you say yes, I say, "How did you choose?" The thought just appeared, "Yes, I feel like it, so I'll go to a movie." Who is in there choosing? Did you create the thought, "Yes, I will go"?

⁜

That just appeared, right? You didn't choose. The answer was "yes." Did you create that yes?

⁜

You didn't choose, did you? The answer was "yes." First there is one thought that says, "Maybe I will go to a movie," that just appears, and then the next thought just appears, "Yes, I feel like it."

Those are just thoughts, aren't they? Did you create those thoughts?

It could just as well have been, "No, I don't feel like it." And that thought would have just appeared. Where in this is there a "you" doing anything? A little you saying, "I am going to create this choice, I am going to choose." Have a holiday and see this.

There is no "you" in there creating. It's just what's going on in the brain, thoughts. See if this is true in your own experience.

It's just what is going on, thought after thought after thought.

Inquirer: *So, free will doesn't exist?*

Sal: If there is no one in here, then who is to have free will? Let's say, the thought comes, "Yes, I will go." Then the next thought is, "I chose to go to a movie." Didn't that thought just appear? "I chose to go to a movie." It's just another thought isn't it?

Inquirer: *Yes.*

Sal: "I could have chosen no, but I chose yes," is another thought, isn't it? You didn't create that thought, did you? It just appeared in this mind. Why? Because this brain is a hard drive and all of the impressions of your life are recorded in there.

There's something called a movie, it's recorded in the brain and then, one day, the brain says, "Maybe I'll go to a movie." It's just what the brain does; it replays what is recorded in there. But then the body/mind doesn't feel like it: "I am too tired." Did you create that you're too tired? If the body/mind says, "Yes, I feel like it," it's just more thoughts, replayed from the impressions that are in the brain. Then the thought comes, "I chose to go to a movie." Isn't this just a thought?

Inquirer: *Yes.*

Sal: Why do you think you're the chooser? Because you've been taught that you're the chooser. They tell you when you're young, "You have free will, you choose what you want to do." That is an uninvestigated assumption. See for yourself if it is true. Don't just believe it.

When you came out of the womb, you were not thinking, "I am going to choose to go to the bathroom." You just went. You're taught that you're the chooser and you have free will, but who says? Because if there's no one in there, there is no one to have free will, is there?

Inquirer: *No.*

Sal: If the answer is, "Yes, I am going to go to a movie," and then you get in your car and you drive, you might say, "I acted, I did the action." But is that action just the logical extension or outcome of the thought intention that appeared? There's a movie, yes, I will go, and then the next thing is the action to do it. There is no one in here doing the action either, it just happens, spontaneously.

There is no doer, there's no chooser, there's no creator and there's no actor. Do you see? And there is no free will. This mind is just replaying what's been put in there. It is only subsequently that we say, "I chose." That is because we believe there is a self in here that can choose. With this inquiry we see that thoughts just appear, and no one is creating them.

There's no "me" in here creating things and choosing. There is no one in here to have free will.

If you fail to notice that you are simply aware of the thoughts and instead believe that those thoughts constitute a "you," then when the thought, "I will go to the movie," appears, you think you made a choice and are the chooser. However, if you look closely, you will observe that thoughts just appear in this body/mind and you are actually just aware of them, just like any other objective appearance.

It's not that you chose those thoughts. They appear, and you mistakenly believe you have something to do with their appearance. If you can recall a time when you had to make a decision that you were unclear about or struggling with, you may recall that in actuality the so-called choice appeared in your awareness at whatever moment it did. It wasn't that you made a choice, but rather that the predominant conclusion just appeared to you (or just appeared in aware), and then you were relieved that you "made a choice." In fact, you just observed the choice/thought/decision as it appeared. There was no chooser, just an awareness of what appeared.

When you recognize that who you are is aware and that this body/mind appears in aware, it becomes clear that it is the identification with the body/mind which leads you to believe that you are the doer, creator, chooser and actor who has free will. Do you recognize what I am saying?

Inquirer: Yes. Everything just happens?

Sal: Yes. But don't take my word for it or believe me. Is it true or not?

Inquirer: Yes, I see that. It's very different from what I have believed.

Sal: Did you create any of the thoughts in your head?

Inquirer: No.

Sal: Furthermore, not only is there not a chooser, there are no choices either. There's not a choice; whatever is, is. It's not a choice, it is what is. See this clearly. Because we say there's a "me" in here, we say, "I chose." But I say, "No, there's no me and there is no choice." See?

Inquirer: Yes. It's very difficult because my whole life I've lived thinking that I do things, I choose, and I have free will.

Sal: Yes, we all do. It's what we're taught. That's the whole problem with the world. This is why the world is such a mess, because everybody thinks they're the doer with free will. Then everyone blames everyone else because they think they're the doer with free will. If I think I am the doer, then I have to think you're also the doer and you're very bad because you did certain things. So then, you have to go to the electric chair.

But who are you? Have a holiday, now.

"Aware," right? Free. Are you a thing, an object? Not a thing, right? If you're not a thing, how could you be a chooser? You're just aware of what's going on. You're just aware that the answer was, "Yes, I'll go to the movie." Aware, who you are, doesn't do anything. Everything is just appearing in some mystery, and it's not understandable to anybody, but it's just the way it works.

Attraction

Here's another example. Let's say you meet someone and you're attracted to them. Did you create that attraction? Did you choose to be attracted to that person?

It just was so, right? So then, because you're attracted to each other, one of you has the thought to ask the other out on a date. Did you create that thought? Or is that just what happened because the attraction was there?

<hr />

Now, you get together and like each other. For some reason, you share many qualities that you both enjoy, physical, intellectual, etc. Did you create that?

<hr />

Your attraction is just natural. Did you create it yourself? You didn't create this attraction, did you? You didn't create the qualities in the other person that attracted you. So then, you get together with this person, and maybe things are good, they're working and you are having a nice time. Did you create that, or is that just the way it's happening? It could have been that you had a bad time.

<hr />

There's something in our culture called marriage. Did you create something called marriage? No. This brain knows about this thing called marriage, and that's what's supposed to happen. Then the thought comes, "Let's get married." Did you create that thought?

❦

You get married. Now you're married, but you haven't created, done, or chosen anything so far. Did you choose to be attracted? Did you choose to like the qualities of the other person? Did you choose to get married? You can say I chose to get married, but is it true? That's just in culture and in your brain. You feel like getting married, but did you create that feeling? No, it's just how you felt. When you're sixty or seventy years old you might say, "I chose to marry that person." And I say, "No, you didn't choose." We don't know why, but that's what happened.

Einstein

Einstein knew that he was not the doer. He was a very smart guy and he also knew something. He said, "I was taking a bath, I wasn't thinking of anything in particular, and all of a sudden E=MC2 came into my head." He said, "I didn't create it, it just appeared." He knew he didn't do it.

Why hasn't that happened to my mind? Well, first, his brain was much more intelligent than mine. Second, he had all that scientific information in his brain and I don't; how could it possibly appear in my brain? It couldn't. Could I create it? No.

But because he had a very highly intelligent brain and all of that data, one day sitting in the bathtub all of a sudden E=MC2 appears, and he said, "I didn't do it." Someone who wasn't so wise would say, "I invented it, I created it, I am so great, I am so smart. I'm the great me, the great doer, the great self." But Einstein said, "No, that's not how it happened."

As a songwriter, I know this very well for myself. I cannot write a song through willpower. If I sit down to write, either there will be a song there or not. And I see that in the midst of it happening, it is just happening, and I am watching it come into being. I can't force it. For whatever reason, this brain has some musical inclination, and I have many years of experience in music. Thus, music can be realized through this person.

Experiment — The Moment You Began Seeking

After reading this experiment, I will ask you to do the same thing for your own experience.

Sal: There was a moment in your life when you became a seeker. Please tell me about that.

> *Inquirer: I just knew that I needed something, but I didn't know what. There was something missing.*

Sal: Why did you know that? What made you know that?

> *Inquirer: I don't know, I just felt like that.*

Sal: You just felt like there was more.

> *Inquirer: Yes.*

Sal: Then you started reading? Meditation?

> *Inquirer: Yes, yoga, reading, lots of courses, Buddhism, meditation, and retreats.*

Sal: When did that happen?

> *Inquirer: Many years ago.*

Sal: You felt there was something missing and you felt there was more. Then you heard about yoga, meditation, and about all these teachers. So, in that moment when you realized there must be something more, did you create that? Or did it just happen?

Inquirer: It just happened.

Sal: Right? Did it happen to your best friend?

Inquirer: No.

Sal: Why?

Inquirer: Because she was not interested. She didn't have the same information.

Sal: The answer is you don't know. Why did it happen to you? You don't know, but it did. So, you didn't choose to become a seeker, did you?

Inquirer: No.

Sal: This is what I am getting to. You did not choose that. You didn't say, "I choose to go for enlightenment." It's just what happened. Then you heard of something called yoga. Did you create yoga?

Inquirer: No.

Sal: Some information went in there and then it sounded interesting to you. Did you create the fact that it sounded interesting?

Inquirer: *No, it just did.*

Sal: So, did you choose to go to yoga, or is it just what happened?

Inquirer: *It just happened.*

Sal: Right, and then you heard of some teachers. Did you create them? Someone may have told you about them and said they were very good and it sounded very interesting. So, you were interested. Did you create this interest?

Inquirer: *No.*

Sal: No, it was just there. You did not choose to become a seeker. You did not choose to connect with teachers. You did not choose to meet me either. You saw a video online and for whatever reason it interested you. You did not create that interest. And because it interested you, you wrote to me and now this is happening.

Now, please go through the same process with your own life. Really do this.

What began your seeking? If you read some books, why did you read those particular books? Did you choose to be interested in those books, or were you just interested? If you had some experiences that pointed to something different, did you create them, or did they just happen? If you became a Buddhist or something else, did you choose to do that or was it just that Buddhism attracted you for some reason? If you are reading this book, then it somehow came into your consciousness. Did you choose for that to happen? And, if you have gotten this far, then something about this book has interested you. Did you create that interest?

Please look into all of these questions thoroughly in your own life experience. Once you have done that then go forward.

⚬⚬⚬

Story

Let's have a little story. Let's say you were born in 1940 in Mississippi and your father and mother were in the Ku Klux Klan. They hated black people, Latinos, and anyone that wasn't white and Christian. This is what you were born into, so these are the impressions that were put into your brain your whole life. It's all you know. You hear that from all of your friends too. When you grow up, who are you most likely going to be?

Inquirer: *A Ku Klux Klan member.*

Sal: Yes, most likely. Would that then be your fault? Would you have chosen it? Someone who believes they are the doer with free will may say, "You could have chosen differently." Really? If, for some reason, the intention for truth didn't appear in your head (and you don't know why it appeared to you), then it didn't appear. Whose fault is it? No one's.

So, how can we blame anyone? How can we judge like this? You can see that the actions are bad, but how can you blame some person, when you know there is no doer and no chooser? Who can we blame?

The point of what we're doing is to see that there's no separate self in here who creates, chooses, and acts out of free will. If the thought or feeling comes that you chose, then know that it's just another thought appearing. It's just one of the impressions in this mind.

It's the same with thinking. We say, "I am thinking." But in truth, there is no thinker and no thinking either, there are just thoughts. I am aware of them, but I am not creating them, they're just appearing. If I think, "Oh, I need to have better thoughts," or "I have to get rid of these bad thoughts," then those are just thoughts appearing. I am just aware of all of them, you see?

You see the same phenomenon when you need to make a decision. We may say, "I am thinking about what to choose," but in reality, we are waiting for the choice to appear to us.

Judgment

You have heard, "You shall not judge!" This is a dogmatic commandment based on the belief that you are the doer, with free will. The fact is, if I know I am not the doer and there is no free will, then I know that it is the same for everyone else, whether they know it or not. So how can I take credit and how can I assign blame? This is the end of judgment. Not because of some teaching that says, "Thou shalt not judge," but because I know what's true.

Once you know the truth, it's very hard to look at someone and judge, although you can say their actions are bad. Dick Cheney and George Bush did some terrible things. But, is it their fault? If there is no free will here, there is no free will there either.

You cannot be anything other than what you are, and it is likewise for everyone else.

Of course, you can look at actions that are harmful and say, "These are bad things." That kind of critical judgment is obviously right. But to say those people are evil, bad and have to be killed in the electric chair, I can't see it that way. They had no choice, there's no chooser and no free will.

One time, Ramana Maharshi was in the ashram with some devotees, and some burglars came. The burglars broke in, robbed them, and they beat Ramana with a stick. (He had a leg injury for the rest of his life from that.) All the devotees wanted to go get these guys and beat them, but Ramana said, "No, they're just acting out their karma, they're just doing what they're supposed to be doing, leave them alone." He wouldn't let his devotees do anything about it, he just sat there while they stole from him and beat him.

There's nothing you can do, there is no chooser. I am not saying to sit there if someone is beating you, that's extreme. If someone is doing something bad, you stop them. If someone is hurting a child in front of me, I am going to stop them. But I also know that this person has no choice, so I stop the bad action, but I don't say, "Bad person, you're going to hell."

Compassion

One of the biggest automatic results of coming to know that there is no free will for you or anyone else is that it elicits compassion. When we know we are not the doer with free will, we also know it to be true for everyone else. True compassion has to apply to all, not just victims. Someone who does terrible things cannot be other than they are, just as you cannot be other than you are. If you did not create yourself then they did not either.

Does that mean we let people do bad things? No, of course not. If someone is harming people, we can't allow them to continue. For now, our system is to put them away in jail. I don't know of a better way, that is what it is for now. Unfortunately, our whole system of justice is based on vengeance and punishment. There is no compassion in that. There is only the belief that a person is bad or evil, they chose to do what they did, and, in fact, they could have chosen differently with their free will. This is an illusion.

I don't know if there was a Jesus, or if so, what he said, but there is a quote attributed to him that indicates he knew this. When they were nailing spikes in his hands and feet, he had compassion. He knew that he had no free will. Why did he want to find truth? He doesn't know. Why don't the people doing this to him want to find truth? He doesn't know. He knows that he did not create himself, and so neither did they. So, he says, "Forgive them; they know not what they do." Jesus knew this compassion, born from the knowing that there is no free will.

⁂

Where do You Want to Live?

Do you want to live in truth, in freedom, or do you want to live in the insane asylum of thoughts and impressions? Do you want to live in the nuthouse, or do you want to live free? Where do you want to live?

It's not a choice either. Just see. It's not, "Now I am going to choose to live free." In the seeing of what is true, it becomes clear to you. It's very natural. The intention is there, but you're not creating the intention. It's the same, no choice, no doer. It is not, "I am now going to do freedom." There is no doer. You've just come to know something. You've had a shift of knowing.

Inquirer: *It's very shocking that there's no doer.*

Sal: Yes, it's shocking. But see for yourself, is it true or not? That's the most important thing, to see for yourself. This is freedom. This is the end of judgment and blame and is the beginning of true compassion. It's the end of pride, like, "I am so great, the great enlightened one." It's not, "Thou shalt not have pride." It's simply that you know what is true, and you can only be who you are. You didn't create yourself, and so what is there to be proud of and who is there to blame?

INQUIRY FOUR: QUESTIONS AND ANSWERS

Is There a Chooser?

> **Inquirer:** *I still have some thoughts about how I found you. My quest, my intense "desire for liberation," it has to be somewhere? I was searching, and I found that YouTube is full of every guru and teacher out there. When I saw you, for some reason, it just clicked, but still, wasn't that kind of a choice? Because I vacillated for a while, a week or so, "Should I? Well okay, what do I have to lose?" And finally, it just came down to that. But if it's not a choice, what inclination led me to choose you?*

Sal: You said that you had this burning desire for liberation. Did you create that desire, or did you just find yourself with that desire happening? My question is: who is the "you" that would choose to find out about liberation? Is there another you in there making choices based on the thoughts that appear? Or does one thought simply "rule the day," so to speak? And for whatever reason, that thought either compels action, or it does not. Or that thought may not appear at all.

In fact, the desire only appeared because your mind heard that it was possible to become liberated. Only then did the desire appear. A bit more of a complete investigation will reveal that the idea just appeared in your mind, based on impressions recorded in it, none of which you can claim. It only appears to have been a choice, subsequently. But if you look clearly, you notice that it's not a choice, it is just what is. It's what appeared there.

Inquirer: I found myself with it happening.

Sal: Right. Then there's something called YouTube, which has a lot of videos on it and which you didn't create. Because of this burning desire, which you did not create, this thought comes, "Let me go on YouTube and look around." Did you create that thought?

Inquirer: My desire for liberation caused me to go on YouTube and look around?

Sal: Your desire? Is there a "you" in there that has a desire, or is there just a desire?

Inquirer: Just a desire.

Sal: Otherwise, there is some "you" inside there, some little soul or self that has a desire. Isn't it just that the desire for liberation is appearing in this mind?

Inquirer: Yes, I would definitely say yes, the desire for liberation is appearing.

Sal: There was no "you" to create that desire. Whatever the circumstances were that led to that desire, you didn't create those either. If you go back and back, you can't find the first thing that you created. You'd have to go back to the Big Bang, and even that you didn't do.

Inquirer: Right.

Sal: Because of that desire, a thought appears, "Go on YouTube." Then you click on a video and it doesn't move you that much. Is it your choice to be moved or not to be moved? If you are not moved, you're just not moved, right?

Inquirer: Just not moved. It doesn't click.

Sal: You didn't choose that, it just doesn't click for you, right? Then for whatever reason, you click on my video, and for some reason, something piqued your interest. Did you create that interest, or did that just happen? "Oh, this is interesting?"

Inquirer: Well, yes, it was interesting. I was obviously attracted.

Sal: Did you create that attraction or it's just what happened in the mind?

Inquirer: It's what happened.

Sal: Then you say you vacillated back and forth. "Oh, that's interesting," and then the next thought was, "Oh, I don't know." Were those thoughts created by you or did they just appear in your mind?

Inquirer: It's what I felt.

Sal: Did you create that feeling?

Inquirer: It was just there.

Sal: Then eventually, the thought or feeling appeared, "Yes, let me write to Sal." Did you create that, or was it that the feeling or thought appeared?

Inquirer: It's a thought that appeared. But still, there was a question. I was still questioning myself. Then the thought that occurred was, "What do I have to lose by doing this?"

Sal: Isn't that just a thought? "What do I have to lose by doing this?"

Inquirer: Yes, a thought.

Sal: Did you create that thought?

Inquirer: No, it was just there.

Sal: Isn't the questioning of yourself just one thought saying, "Yes," and another thought saying, "I don't know," and another thought saying, "Yes, maybe"? Did you create any of those thoughts?

Inquirer: No, no.

Sal: Then eventually, a thought came, "Just write," and so you wrote. Did you create that?

Inquirer: No... I entertained them.

Sal: You entertained them? Where is this "you?" This is where I want to get to now, because, have a look and show me where this "you" is inside—find it.

Inquirer: My brain entertained them? I don't know, something did.

Sal: It was just thoughts appearing, and you were aware of them, right?

Inquirer: The intelligence that I am entertained all the different thoughts that were occurring. Saying, "should I?"

Sal: Why is there someone here who is entertaining things? Isn't it just thoughts going off in this head?

Inquirer: Yeah, it is, but still I exist.

Sal: You exist, but you don't exist as a thing. We've seen, I am not a thing, I am no-thing. If you look in truth, you're not located anywhere, are you? Have a holiday.

⚛

Look, now. Because if you look now, you honestly and genuinely cannot find a self. Where is this "me" who is entertaining things? If there is one, you must be able to find it. Even the thought, "I must be entertaining thoughts," is just appearing. Even the feeling that I feel like I am the doer, isn't that feeling just there, appearing within aware?

Inquirer: That I am the doer?

Sal: Yes, that there is a choice, "I must have chosen." Isn't that just a thought? "I must have chosen" just appears in your head. So, why is this confusion or doubt happening? Did you create it or is it just appearing, now?

> **Inquirer:** *I guess I am trying to over-analyze the situation. It's not that I doubt, I don't doubt at all. But there is that other part of me that's always believed there was a soul or some kind of a continuum of energy that carries us. I don't think that when we leave this life that we just don't exist, I think there's a continuum.*

Sal: Who carries on or who would not exist? Who's this "I" that allegedly exists?

> **Inquirer:** *The thing that carries us on. We gain experience from situations and we learn and we grow, as a soul, as energy, or whatever. There has to be that intelligence that we're able to draw on. It can be experiences or things and we go on from there. Do you know what I mean?*

Sal: At the root of all of these questions is the belief that there's a separate "me" in here that is the controller, the doer, the experiencer.

Inquirer: That would be like the ego, the personality, whatever.

Sal: Yes, self, the soul or something. The "me" that's here in this body. That's the root of these questions. I can't find that. You have to look in your own experience, not in what you believe, or what you've heard or read, but in your own experience, right now. See? You would never have thought there's a soul if you hadn't read or heard that there's something called a soul. How could you have ever come up with that one, right?

Inquirer: I know, and this is all about liberation, and I see the liberation thing. I see that without getting rid of these structured, rigid ideas we have, that we're just clinging on to the I-ness, to the "me, me, me." In order to be liberated, that's got to be released.

Sal: It doesn't have to be released, truth has to be known. You have to know what's true. There's nothing to release. Who is going to release anything? There's a knowing that's not separate from aware, not separate from who I am, but it's not a personal thing. This knowing, knows itself as aware and free. So, nothing has to be let go of. It's "Know what's true, and truth will set you free." It's not, "Let go of beliefs and the letting go will set you free." It doesn't say that. It's "know."

We simply see clearly that we haven't created any of these thoughts, they're just appearing. Is this true or am I making that up?

Inquirer: *It's true.*

Sal: Is there a creator in here creating thoughts? When you came out of the womb, did you have the idea that there is a soul? There is an afterlife? Did you have those ideas?

Inquirer: *No.*

Sal: A soul, and the question, "What am I going to do after I die?" No, you didn't have them. You were a blank slate, weren't you? The basic operating system was there, the five senses and consciousness. Then, the computer started collecting data, and beliefs—there's a soul, there's a "me" in here. This is just data, isn't it?

Inquirer: *Yes.*

Sal: This data is stored in the brain and it replays this data as thoughts, ideas, concepts, and beliefs. Where in all of that is there a "me" creating any of it?

Inquirer: *Nowhere.*

Sal: There isn't. You didn't create the thought of a soul, that was an idea put into your computer. Now, all of a sudden, this, who I am, freely aware, all-inclusive, this knowing, makes a mistake (the original sin) and says, "I am this, this thought stream, the amalgamation of concepts and ideas. This is who I am. I am this body." You make a mistake and think, "I am this body and collection of thoughts," exclusively.

We believe the data in our brain, we believe there is something called the soul. But you can't find the soul. There's no empirical evidence that it exists, yet, as a belief, you take it on that there's a soul in here because you don't want to give up self for anything. You don't want to give up this ego existence for anything, so you have to invent the afterlife. Because then you can live forever, in eternity.

To give those things up means you don't know what's going to happen after death. I think, and I could be wrong, nothing happens. This personalized consciousness is simply finished. The only thing that dies is the belief in self. This is why most people don't come to liberation, because they're not ready.

Inquirer: *I can imagine it would be very difficult for someone who is very egocentric.*

Sal: I say the belief in a soul is extremely egocentric. It doesn't really get more egocentric than that. "I have a soul and it's going to live forever." That's about as egocentric as it gets. Have a holiday and see if you can find a soul anywhere.

☙❧

Can I Choose to Not be Lost in Stories?

Inquirer: In the beginning of recognition, it seems that it's a matter of choice. Is there a choice to not be lost in stories?

Sal: First of all, choice implies that there's a chooser. I say, "There's no choice." There's no such thing as choice and there's no such thing as free will. Free will is the same as choice. Free will implies someone who has free will, choice implies someone who is choosing. But, if we see there's no one in here, then where is the question of choice or free will? What is, is. Liberation means knowing, "What is, is," doubtlessly. In the moment you recognize that you're so-called "lost in a story" and you see something different, did you do that, or did it just happen?

Inquirer: Well, if you say let's have a holiday, is that going to automatically kick in? It seems like

I'm seeing all the impressions, and I choose to have a holiday.

Sal: First of all, "Have a holiday" is not something you created. I put that seed into your head, that's an impression, a thought, and then in the midst of thinking, "Have a holiday" appears. I say you didn't choose that.

Inquirer: *Because it's in my field, it's in my space.*

Sal: It's just a thought in your head. You're fully attending to thoughts and then another thought appears, "Have a holiday." You didn't create that thought, did you?

Inquirer: *No, it's there.*

Sal: You didn't create its arising in that moment. In the midst of a story, all of a sudden, "Have a holiday" appears, doesn't it? If that is true, then did you choose to have a holiday? I say, no.

There's no criticism if you're lost in stories for a day, a week or a month. It doesn't matter because even if it's a month, when a holiday happens, what's changed? Nothing. You're still here, free, as you've always been. An hour, a day or a month, it doesn't matter. There's no good or bad student.

Even if you're "lost in stories," you're still free, because you are free.

Recognizing truth takes no time, but liberating this mind from seeking takes time because the momentum of belief has been going on our whole lifetime and this takes some time to resolve. It's not at all realistic to expect that to happen immediately. Go easy on yourself. I don't know the moment when I knew it was over. There wasn't any specific experience or moment, it was just in hindsight, I realized, "Oh it's over." There wasn't any particular moment.

> **Inquirer:** *So, there is that moment, that realization or recognition that it's over.*

Sal: Maybe not, it doesn't matter. There's no specific goal. You'll know. There's no goal that you should be looking for in the future, forget that. Have a look, now. You are free.

⟨∽≋⟩

Fear

> **Inquirer:** *I have an example, last night I received some news that the son of friends of ours, while on a trip, developed flu symptoms, and they got worse. Actually, it was a virus that*

created meningitis, it went to the brain and he went into a coma and died within two days. Totally unexpected.

I just heard this last night, "How do I deal with this?" I moved into sadness and then a place of fearing, for my family, for myself and others. I don't have freedom around that fear, about something happening to the physical body and my loved ones. I don't like living in fear.

Sal: Is there anything wrong with those emotions appearing, or is it very natural?

Inquirer: *I'd say it's probably pretty natural. But, almost every day, when my husband leaves for work (he has a long commute, there's a lot of deer on the highways, and the roads are bad), I get into a place of fearing for him, fearing for my family members, and fearing for myself.*

I live in fear too much. I don't have that in check, in balance or whatever. I think it's natural to have some of those fears but not to live in that fear all the time. So, I have a judgment about it.

Sal: Ok. But, in the moment of that fear, isn't that fear true? That's what's appearing, now, right?

Inquirer: *Yes.*

Sal: If that's what's appearing, now, then the belief that it shouldn't be appearing or that you should be able to deal with it somewhat better is called becoming, and it's a lie.

Inquirer: *And that perpetuates it?*

Sal: It makes you spin off into other tangents around that fear and that keeps the whole thing going. Why do you think that that fear is not natural? The reason is, for one thing, spiritual teachings tell you that you should be equanimous—you should always be in bliss, no matter what's appearing. This is nonsense. The reason you think there is something wrong with your experience of fear, or that you're not enlightened and you're doing something wrong is because you've been taught to believe that. In truth, if fear is appearing, it's very natural and it's true. It's what is, here and now.

The work we're doing together is not to get rid of anything that's appearing, that would be impossible. You didn't create that fear, did you? If you didn't create it, then you can't get rid of it either.

Inquirer: The other me thinks that I created it,
so I can uncreate it.

Sal: The "other me" is just another thought that has been impressed in your mind, it's just a belief. Your culture tells you that you're in control, you're the doer and you've got to take charge of your emotions. This is what's been taught to you, but it's not true. You'll find out for yourself. You've been taught to believe that you can control this fear or that you should control it—that there is an autonomous person inside here that's creating things and doing things. That's just another belief, another thought.

So then, what happens? There's no empirical self that has been here since we were born because many times a day we default to this free condition. When we identify with form, self appears, and then it resolves again to the default free condition. In the moment of fear, you are fear. That's what self is in that moment, fear. There's not another "you" in here having fear. If that was true, there would be the fear plus the one in here who's having the fear. But this is not what's happening, what's happening is that in the moment of fear, I am fear.

Here is a metaphor. Ocean is flat. In the moment of a wave, the wave is ocean, isn't it? And this ocean is wave and this wave may be fear. In the moment the wave of fear is appearing, ocean is appearing as fear. Then the wave resolves, and ocean hasn't changed at all.

So, because we're taught to believe that there is a controller, a creator, and a doer in here, what we do when fear appears, is we split ourselves in two—the fear and then the one who can do something about it. We're creating two where, in fact, there is none. There is no one, there's only the appearance of fear and, in that moment, that's what self is appearing as. In the next moment, self may be appearing as happiness, and in the next moment, it may be appearing as worry, concern, sadness, joy, or peace. That's what you are appearing as, in the moment, just like ocean is appearing as wave. But you're taught to think that there is another one of you in there that needs to do something about that.

Inquirer: *Yes, that I am in charge.*

Sal: Yes, that you're in charge. But that's not the way it's working, it is just a belief. It creates separation within yourself, a duality. It propagates the belief that there's something you can do, and you have to get in there and fix it. Then it spins out into other stories about how bad or stupid you are, and how you are not getting anywhere, and if you get in there and resolve it, it's going to be fine. But then this wave doesn't get to resolve naturally.

What I am saying here is that what is, is, and you didn't create it, it appears by itself. It's just appearing, and it's very natural. Not only that, it's true. Because in this moment, there is fear, you can't deny it. If you deny it, you are denying what is. If you try to say, "I've got to get rid of this, I am not enlightened, and I have to resolve this," it is a lie because what's true is fear is appearing. Liberation means we stop arguing with what is.

Do you think I am always in peace and bliss or something like that? No. If something bad happens to a loved one, do I feel something? Of course, I do. This body/mind organism gets touched, doesn't it? By loved ones, by their joys, by their sorrows, by things that happen, there's an emotional element going on, isn't there? There is an empathetic component in this body. Why would we argue with that? That's how this body/mind operates.

Liberation is the end of trying to change what is or seek for something other than what is. The end of seeking, the end of becoming other than what I am, right now.

Anything can appear for me, but I don't think there's something wrong with me because of it. The wave comes and then it goes—very natural. It doesn't come and go when you get in there and think, "There's something wrong with me and I have to resolve it." The wave gets bigger and bigger the more you get in there. The wave gets bigger, and it turns into a tidal wave, and a tsunami. People go through their whole life as a tsunami of emotions because they just keep feeding it with the belief that it means something, about them, that they created it, that they can change it, and that they have to do something about it. This is suffering.

In liberation, we just know, a wave comes, and a wave goes. Everything passes. Businesses come, and businesses are going to end, it's inevitable, whether it is now, next week, or next year. Whatever comes always goes. Nothing lasts forever, including a business. It's just truth. And this is true of people too. People come and go. You cannot argue with that. So why bother?

What comes comes, and what comes goes. I've lost many things in my life, gained and lost, gained and lost. That's the way it is. Know what's true. Nothing lasts forever. If we start holding on, thinking, "All things shall pass except this business," then we're going to suffer when it does pass, which is inevitable. And if someone is suffering, then that is what is.

By seeing truth clearly, it resolves our mind's attempts to change and fix what is, and our thinking that there's something wrong with "me" because of what's appearing. When we are reconciled with what is, is, the ocean is just flowing very nicely, the ocean of life. Wave after wave— happiness, sadness, fear, joy, winning, losing, gaining, etc. Isn't that the way life works?

These fears that you have about your family, you can't argue with them because they are appearing. But if you stop arguing with them, they will lose a lot of power. Because when you argue with something like that, it gives it power. The on switch to the power is the belief that it means something, that it's wrong, and that it needs to change. That right there will propagate it forever because it gives it juice.

It's a belief in self. You're going into the carousel of mind, of psychology. You think, "Oh no, there's fear, it's not good, it's wrong and I've been taught that I've got to control it. I created it and I am not so enlightened." This is just propagating the belief in ego/self.

What is, is. Just know that and be finished. I don't say, "Let it be as it is" or "Don't be attached." I don't say those things because there is no one to let everything be as it is. There is just another thought saying this, and this thought is your conditioning.

Inquirer: *Or let it go.*

Sal: Let it go also. There is no one in here to do any of this. We're creating a self, the other self that's going to let something go, or let something be as it is, or be not attached. This is creation of another self, just another thought. I say it differently: Know that what is, is. And be finished arguing.

Can you argue with that? What is, is. Is that true?

Inquirer: *That's true.*

Sal: Okay, then stop arguing. There's nothing wrong with you because fear appears. That's what we're taught, "Oh, there is fear, so go and see a therapist."

Inquirer: *The famous word now is intention. So, set your intention.*

Sal: Yes, you have an intention, which is in there. You didn't create it, but for some reason that intention appeared in your mind, like the intention for truth and freedom. That's why we're speaking together, because that intention appeared. You already know what freedom is and that intention can lead to liberation of this mind. And again, liberation is just knowing that what is, is. It's the end of arguing with it, it's the peace that passes understanding.

You can see how much conditioning is in your mind from culture that goes against what I just said. Culture says, you have to change, create, resolve and fix. It's just creating another self in there that has responsibility, but you didn't create any of it. Those are just thoughts and beliefs. It's nothing; it's just in there. We're not trying to get rid of that, not even that belief. Just know what's true, and truth will set you free.

I put a little seed in your head. In the midst of these fears, for a moment, have a holiday and know something—I am aware, who I am is free, life itself, here and now, already and always have been. You just know this again. Have another "aha" moment. Just for a few seconds.

Don't try to get rid of anything or relieve anything. Just to see, for a moment, that when there is fear, truth is still true. If you do this, fear will subside on its own.

Have a holiday now and see again that you're free.

Please go through Inquiry Four again thoroughly. Take a few days to see that there is no doer in your own experience, before you move on. Whenever a thought, intention, desire or anything appears, see that it just appeared from nowhere.

INQUIRY FIVE — FREE FROM SUFFERING

Using Strategies of Avoidance

What does it mean to be free from suffering? Does it mean that we will never experience anything unpleasant or painful, either physically or emotionally? Seekers have the idea that they are going to arrive at a place or state of consciousness where they will always feel good, or they will be in a state of equanimity where they are never affected by anything negative.

This body/mind organism is the experiencing entity. You, freely aware, are aware of the experiences of this body/mind organism. Have a holiday. See that you are aware of the body and the thoughts in it. They appear to you just like any other object in aware. Do this now, for a moment.

❦

This body/mind organism has the ability to experience so-called negative emotions and sensations. If it was not meant to experience them, it wouldn't. If it was only intended to have pleasant experiences, then that is all it would have. But that is not what is true, is it?

If you stick a pin in your arm, it hurts. If a loved one dies, it causes sadness. If you see someone being cruel to someone else, you feel sympathy. If you see someone harming a child, anger arises. This is all natural, isn't it? So, why do we argue with it and think it should be any different or that it will be different once we get enlightened?

We use many strategies to avoid feeling bad. We deny, ignore, mask, replace negative with positive, anesthetize with drugs or alcohol, distract ourselves with entertainment, etc.— anything to not feel bad. Spiritual seekers do the same thing— we meditate and try to stop our mind from thinking, we try to get some bliss or other spiritual experiences. We are trying to escape our humanity because sometimes it doesn't feel good to be human. But it never ultimately works, does it?

We spend our whole life trying to arrange our circumstances, including our thoughts and emotions, so that we're comfortable. We want more money and a perfectly flawless relationship. We want eternal good health, circumstances that make us feel safe and never have fear, and we want to have only pleasant thoughts and emotions.

We have been relying on and arranging circumstances and appearances so that we don't suffer. It doesn't work. Let's face it, life is not just filled with pleasant circumstances and feelings. To deny that would be untrue. But we've been trying to avoid unpleasant experiences in the hope that we will be free of suffering.

What happens if you don't use any strategies of avoidance or control? Then when something unpleasant happens, you will just feel bad, for a while. It is perfectly natural. Without the resistance of avoidance and these other strategies, it will flow by naturally, and it will usually flow by quickly too.

We turn the emotion into a problem by using these strategies and add on to it, causing it to not resolve or flow by naturally. We give this emotion too much power by valuing it and believing it means something important, or that it is wrong to feel it and it must indicate something like, I am unenlightened.

The peace that passes understanding is not a state of peace or bliss. What is in this moment cannot be any different than it is now. To stop denying or arguing with what is, is peace. If it is pleasant it is pleasant, if it is not pleasant it is not pleasant. To deny what is, is a false view, which causes resistance and suffering. There is a lot of relief in not denying or arguing with what is, whether it is pleasant or unpleasant. Then you are not fighting within yourself.

When you hear that you can be free from suffering, you get the idea that you are never going to feel bad. But is that true? There is nothing you can do about a painful or unpleasant appearance. Why? You have already seen that there is no doer here and no one creating anything. Whatever appears, appears, spontaneously. And whatever is appearing must be true, because it is.

Yes, you can say that a painful emotion or physical event is suffering. There is nothing you can do about that. The suffering you can be free of is the suffering caused by all of the unnecessary resistance and pressure you add on by using strategies of avoidance. There is the original pain and now added on to that is the denial and resistance, which propagates, reifies and causes the pain to amplify and last longer than it needs to.

We create stories and tell ourselves, "Poor me," which adds on to the emotion. These stories keep the emotion alive by reliving them many times, again and again. This kind of suffering can end. This is the suffering you can be free of.

In the middle of an emotional upset, have a holiday. See that your essential being is already free from suffering. Don't try to do anything about the emotional discomfort. Having a holiday will keep you from propagating the story and also from trying to cover up or avoid the pain. Then see that it passes naturally on its own without you doing anything.

Know that it is perfectly natural to experience both pleasant and unpleasant things. Don't expect that you should or will ever come to a place where that doesn't happen. Reconciling this is being free from suffering.

❧

True Confidence

We all want confidence, but we base our sense of confidence on appearances. If we have a lot of money and look good, or if we are popular and successful, we feel confident. Those things can, and will, all go. You can lose your money or looks.

I heard about someone in Washington D.C. who was a big politico; going to parties with Bill Clinton, making a lot of money, living in a big house, etc. He was a popular person and had a lot of confidence because of that. Then he lost it all and has been insecure ever since. He based all of his self-worth and confidence on what he had.

This kind of confidence is flimsy, and it can also bring about arrogance and bravado, a puffed-up confidence. This kind of confidence can be even malignant in the worst case. Have a holiday, now.

You know who you are—aware and free, lacking nothing, complete and whole already. This is the true confidence. It is not based on any appearance, or on what you have. It is totally benign and humble. It has nothing to prove, nothing to gain, and nothing to lose. It doesn't change. You can look anyone in the eyes, and be space for them to be, with benign, humble confidence.

INQUIRY FIVE: QUESTIONS AND ANSWERS

Self Blame

> **Inquirer:** *I've had some ear pain and the thought sometimes arises that I did something wrong. I don't recognize this is just what's happening.*

Sal: This notion that you did something wrong and that is why something is happening to you has been programmed into your brain (all our brains) by culture, through religion or psychology. This emanates from the notion that there is free will.

Also, we use our experiences as a barometer for how we're doing. We say, "Today I had pleasant sensations or circumstances, so I am doing great." If someone says to me, "Oh, I am doing great," I think, "Nice, talk to me tomorrow, because tomorrow you may not feel so well." We judge how we are by the current experience. As goes the experience, so go I.

That's what we've been taught to do, and by doing that, we create suffering because we get into the story of it.

Knowing what's true cuts off the story of suffering, which is the real suffering. That's the suffering we can cut. We can't stop painful experiences and we can't stop painful emotional experiences. You can say that those are suffering, and I agree. If something is happening that is very unpleasant, physically or emotionally, we can call it suffering. However, we can't do anything about that, can we? Because whatever appears, appears. By coming to know what's true, we don't propagate that into stories that create extra unnecessary suffering.

In the midst of something that's not pleasant, you want truth, and there's nothing to do but know. Because you want truth, you won't go into the story. Not that you should or shouldn't, you just won't because you want truth.

Often, the problem is not what's happening. It's that we think there is something that is the source of the suffering. It is the story in our mind that accompanies the event that is the cause of unnecessary suffering. That kind of suffering can end, the story suffering. The physical and emotional discomfort or pain will come and go. It's the natural function of the body. Who am I to argue with this?

The peace that passes understanding, from the Bible, is not peace and bliss. It's the end of arguing with what is, whether it's good or bad, positive or negative, pleasant or unpleasant, etc. It's the end of arguing with what is.

Inquirer: *This eliminates blame and all that.*

Sal: That's right.

Inquirer: *I see what you mean when you say, "It's stark and all there is, is now." What's appearing is it.*

Sal: Right. I don't use the word acceptance, and I don't say, "Accept what is" because then there's a doer in there, an acceptor, "I am the great acceptor of what is." A liberated person is fully reconciled that what is can be no other way than it is, now. What is, is. There's no argument. There's no doer. Just being fully reconciled.

INQUIRY SIX — EGO

Eight False Evidences of self

The Five Senses

There are eight things that we believe are proof that there is a self. The first five are the senses—seeing, hearing, touching, tasting, and smelling. "I see the tree, so that is proof that I am here, separate." Let's have a holiday, now. Look at any object in your room.

❧

Your eyes work perfectly without a "you" in there doing anything, don't they? Don't attend to the feeling of self here and see that the object simply is. The eyes work perfectly well; you don't need to claim that there is a seer here for them to see and for the object to be. Have a look.

❧

Is there a "you" needed for seeing to happen, or is seeing just happening because that is what the eyes do? Seeing is happening, period. You add the belief that there is a self in there seeing. This belief seems to be proof that there is a "me" seeing. But the eyes function perfectly well without a "you." Same with all the other senses. Look into this for a while and see for yourself.

We believe there is a perceiver, perceiving the perceived. That is not what is actually happening. There is only perceiving happening in aware. There is not a seer separate from the seen.

If we look into each sense in this way, we see that none of the senses prove that there is a self. There is just seeing, hearing, touching, tasting, and smelling happening, no one is here doing them.

Thoughts and Emotions

Thoughts and emotions seem to be even more compelling evidence that there is a self here. Because thoughts and emotions appear, we believe that there is an "I" in there thinking or feeling them, especially when there are strong emotions or thoughts. In truth, thoughts are just the replaying of impressions recorded in the brain, and emotions are just the physical response to those thoughts or the physical response to events that occur. This is a very natural function of this body/mind. It happens spontaneously, with no creator of them. As we saw in the previous chapter, they appear in empty mind.

Descartes said, "I think, therefore I am." That is incorrect. First, "I think," is wrong. There is no "I" in here to think, as in a verb. There are only thoughts. The belief that there is a thinker in here is simply another thought, which appears spontaneously, because that is what we have been taught to believe. Second, "therefore I am," is also wrong. In the absence of thoughts, I still am. No thought is needed for me to be. In deep, dreamless sleep, I still am.

Emotions such as "I feel terrible," are even more compelling. In truth, there is just a feeling appearing. If someone you love dies, it is natural for sadness to arise. Why would it not? It is simply how this body/mind operates.

These thoughts and emotions appear independently of anyone in here creating them. Thoughts and emotions are not evidence there is a self in here. They just arise and subside in and to aware.

Have a look into this and see if it is true.

❦

Consciousness

The eighth apparent evidence is the most fundamental—consciousness. Consciousness is simply a function of this form that allows knowing. When this body appears, consciousness appears with it. When it wakes up in the morning, consciousness, the knowing function, appears. When consciousness is present, it seems to indicate that there is a separate self who is conscious.

Consciousness does not prove there is a self here. Yes, it feels personal because I can only know the consciousness in this body. I can't know the consciousness in another body, but consciousness is just a function. Consciousness does not prove there is an individual self here.

You are aware of all of those eight apparent evidences—senses, thoughts, emotions, and consciousness. They are all experiences that you know. So, they are objects of knowing. If you are aware of all of them, then you must be before, during, and after they appear. Even the idea or felt sense of self, you are aware of. You identify with those objects and claim them as who you are. None of those objects, however, prove that there is self here, they are simply appearances appearing within this body/mind to you who is aware.

⌁

Transcending the Ego

We have heard we are supposed to transcend the self or kill the ego, but how can we do that without even knowing what it really is? Self is simply the amalgamation of thoughts and beliefs about who you are, the idea that you are the impressions in your mind, your personal history, and future aspirations (becoming). But none of this is actual now, is it? If you are very honest, brutally honest, you have to admit that all of that past and future stuff is a fantasy happening in your mind because now, it simply is not actual.

There is also the feeling in the body that says, "I am here, conscious." This felt sense of I that is appearing now, won't stop happening. Why should it? There is the idea that somehow this sense or feeling of "I am here, conscious, now" is going to go away. We are not trying to get rid of that sense. Yet, know that many times each day there is no felt sense of self—you are not aware of yourself. This is a very normal and natural occurrence. And then, many other times a day, you do have a felt sense of self. This is also very normal and natural. It is in no way in opposition to liberation.

This felt sense of self is not something that is always here, is it? It is an experience that comes and goes like all other experiences. It is simply a wave appearing and disappearing on the surface of ocean, the absolute, your essential aware nature. So, in this way, in the moment of the felt sense of self, it is actual and there is nothing wrong with it.

How does our recognition that there is only now factor into the dissolution of personal history?

As we have seen, there is only now. There is only now, and if we are ready to be real here, then, in truth, nothing ever happened in the past. Recognizing there is only now, you recognize there is no past—there is the idea of a past that exists now in the mind, but the past does not exist in actuality. So, your personal poor me or wonderful me stories, or all of your sentimental stories, are unreal. They are not real. What is real is what is NOW. In truth, you have no history.

If you want to get real, then see what is actual, what is true. Your story of me, this self character, like a character in a movie, has a history. But you, who you are essentially, have no history. All you can say, in truth, is that, here and now, I am.

Nothing more. Are you ready to be reconciled with that? Take a few minutes and look into what is being pointed to.

❧

Seeing this for yourself, knowing it's truth and being reconciled with it, is what it means to kill the ego, to transcend self. Nothing disappears because there is no actual, empirical self/ego here to disappear. Nothing dies because there is no actual ego entity that exists in the first place. This is being free from ego.

It doesn't mean that a felt sense of self, thoughts about the past, or your personal history won't arise—they are coming and going like waves. What it means is that those appearances come and go, and you remain, before, during and after—aware, free, now—always.

Freedom from ego is already attained, here and now. If you ignore the thoughts, ignore the sensations in the body, and ignore the stories about past and future, see that there is no ego. Look now and see.

❧

You have heard how formidable the ego is, how huge, solid, and pervasive it is. You need to be Hercules to kill it and there is little chance you ever will. This is what you have come to believe, and it is understandable because you have been taught it through ignorance and you have not yet seen another way. But now, have a holiday and see.

Where is the beast? Where is ego? It's nothing, isn't it? Ego is a belief. "Oh, I have a such a big ego." "My ego is hurt." "My ego is so complicated." "I can't get enlightened because my ego is in the way." Why tell yourself these stories? Why create a monster that has no actual existence and then fear it and be controlled by it, by a belief?

Someone who is ready to be free from ego is ready, for whatever reason, to give up the belief in ego, the belief in enlightenment in the future, etc. Someone who is ready, is ready to know one thing only, "Here and now, I am." And to see that this is true, and that this is freedom.

I have no idea what happens after death, I don't know why I am here, and I don't know what will happen next. I don't know any of these things. The only thing I know, and the only truthful thing I can say is, "Here and now, I am." I don't know what I am, as in an object. But I do know I am, here and now, free. The only knowing is now.

This is jumping off the carousels of mind, and of ego. If you are ready to be honest, you will stop believing in fairy tales about heaven and hell and what happens after death, nirvana and enlightenment in the future, and your past history and future becoming. And you will admit that the only thing you know is that, here and now, you are. You will not need to believe those things ever again. This is freedom from ego.

There is no doer, so there is nothing to do about it. When a person is mature and ready, it will happen. It will be finished. See that it is finished for you, now.

❧

Playing Ego

It is like we saw earlier about Romeo and Juliet. The actor knows he is an actor, but he does not get off the stage because he knows. He stays on stage and plays his role, knowing fully that it is a play. Ego just appears as it does to someone else, no problem. It is just a play.

We are not trying to become some amorphous blob of egolessness that just sits there and doesn't move. That is an extreme view, which is not what liberation is. You are you. By that, I mean you are not only your essential free nature, but also the character you play in life, which is the totality of impressions and experiences recorded in your mind. You can only be you; there is no other possibility. The experiences and impressions of your life are completely unique, no one can be you and you can't be anyone else.

There is a big difference when you believe in ego, and that you are separate. This can be malignant. Why? Because then you have to protect and defend your ego—be right, prove your point, convince others of your beliefs, and judge others based on the belief in free will. Look at the state of the world to see this. That is why there is war and havoc in interpersonal relationships. But, when you know that ego is just a game, you still play your role, but you don't need to be right, defend your position, convince others of your beliefs or judge others harshly. In this way, ego becomes much more benign.

INQUIRY SIX: QUESTIONS AND ANSWERS

Judgment is self

> **Inquirer:** *It seems like judgment is creating another self.*

Sal: Actually, you are not creating another self. It just seems as though there is another self in there judging whatever the thoughts are. But those are just more thoughts, which have been programmed into your mind by culture and religion. You identify with both the judgment thoughts and the other thoughts they are judging.

> **Inquirer:** *I got annoyed with someone the other day and then quickly realized I wasn't mad anymore.*

Sal: Yes, feelings just flow by. We are human, thoughts and emotions appear, circumstances appear. What we are doing together is the end of trying to transcend our humanity. If you are feeling guilty or think there is something wrong with you because you got annoyed and you need to be more equanimous and enlightened, then there is another "self" in there judging. But those are just more spontaneous thoughts, which have been programmed in your mind, "You are bad for not being equanimous." This can be finished. As you said, annoyance came and then it went, and you were not mad anymore. That is natural, the natural flow of life. Waves come, and then they go, sometimes they are warm, sometimes they are cold, sometimes big and sometimes small.

You've heard on the path that you have to kill the ego or transcend the self. If you believe that, then clearly you believe there is ego/self. How can you kill something that is not actual? It would be like killing Santa Claus. To believe you have to kill the ego supports the belief in separation, that there is in fact an ego that is a discrete object.

As we have seen, self is just an appearance, like a wave. In this moment, some annoyance is appearing, and if you identify with it, then that is self in that moment. Having a holiday and defaulting to the natural free condition, you see, again, in truth, that there is no self. Self needs the concept of time and the belief that the appearance of emotion indicates a "me" here. If you believe in a self, then you believe you have to do something about the appearances.

The default condition, for everyone, is free. Free of self. Many times each day, we default to no identification as a self. However, for most people, when this happens, there is no recognition of what's true (I am free, all-inclusive, now, aware), so it has no ability to end the incessant need to seek and become.

When you have a holiday, know what is true—who I am is aware, free. Value this. It is the natural human condition. This knowing, and valuing it, is what will liberate this mind from seeking.

> **Inquirer:** *If you aren't feeling free, just take another holiday?*

Sal: Freedom isn't a feeling. It is the natural human condition, which you come to know in a holiday, no matter what the feeling is. It has always been true, you just didn't notice until now.

As I said in the beginning of this work, it is like a house of cards. The first card is the belief that I am separate, and all of the other cards are built on top of that. All we need to do is remove the first card.

When we have a holiday, we are just removing that first card. Have a holiday now and see what I mean.

❧

Where is this ego? Don't identify and say I am this body or these thoughts. Just leave that all behind and look now. Who I am is free. Ego means the belief that I am separate. Leave that all behind. Have a holiday. Your nature is aware, free, all-inclusive. Look now. Where is that identification, now?

Inquirer: *There isn't any.*

Sal: Right, we have removed that first card. We have jumped off that carousel. Here and now, I am free, and it has always been true. If I had been able to notice before, I would have recognized the same thing. We are seeing what is true—this belief that there is a discrete self that has an empirical truth to it, and has been here our whole life, is simply a passing ephemeral wave. The only thing that keeps us in so-called bondage to this "ego" is the belief that there is a real self/ego structure, with all of its psychological and philosophical ideas, its past history, and its future hopes and becomings. The belief that this has some validity and power is what keeps us in seeking. We are coming to see that this is simply a belief that is not true; I am not the sum of the impressions in this brain.

We have a shift of knowing and come to know something different. We come to see that that is not who I am. Who I am is free, aware, all-inclusive, unborn, life itself—this is my essential being. Like the belief in Santa Claus, the belief in ego is based upon a false notion. Until we were seven, there wasn't even a question, we just took it for granted that there was a Santa Claus. We had no proof, but we believed it anyway. Then we found out that there is no Santa and the belief was gone. Santa Claus didn't go away because there is no Santa Claus. The only thing that changed is that a belief fell away. It is permanent; you can't believe there is a Santa anymore.

It is the same with this, the recognition that there is no ego is permanent. You now know that there is only now, so these beliefs in the past and future have no validity. Therefore, they have much less, or no, power to cause you to suffer. Those things are just fantasy, they are not actual, now. This is freedom.

It takes a very mature person to live this way because most people are not ready for those beliefs to die. The beliefs give them a false sense of security, a false sense of who they are. It is very flimsy because there is no truth to it.

The only truth is now, and now, there is no ego. In the way I speak about it, someone who is mature, is fully reconciled with this.

What is required for this full reckoning is valuing truth—I lack nothing, I am complete and whole already. Knowing the value of all those things we looked into earlier. Valuing truth is the difference between freedom and ideas of bondage. By continuing to value truth, this full reckoning is possible, it will be finished. It will be doubtless, just like it is doubtless that there is no Santa Claus.

With Santa Claus you don't have to keep looking up the chimney to make sure, because you know he doesn't exist. For now, with this work, because these beliefs in self are deeply ingrained, just keep having holidays and knowing what is true. This knowing and the valuing of it will resolve it. This is not a goal, it just does it automatically.

If you still have the desire to believe in your stories, then you will do that forever. But, if you are mature and ready to be free, then the belief can't last for long. Let's face it, most people won't give up their belief in self because there's nothing in it for them.

This so-called self doesn't get enlightened. It is just seen to be insubstantial, a story, nothing more. No one is getting enlightened; the natural human condition is free. The only thing we know is now, that is the only true knowing. It is not intellectual. This knowing is aware; they are synonyms. Any other knowledge, spiritual, esoteric, mystical, is just ignorance. Just be finished with it all.

All of these beliefs, merging with the divine, spirituality, etc., are just a bunch of fairy tales for adults. Where is any of it, now? They are just more stories, like Santa Claus. A mature person is finished with these fairy tales. Just ordinary life as it is with whatever is appearing.

We have placed inordinate value on this ever changing, dying, disintegrating form and thought structure. We seek security in the ever-changing appearances. But there is no real security in that. The true security is only now; this knowing that is aware and never changes. This is fully jumping off the carousels of mind. This is a huge relief, to be finished with these fairy tales, the past and the future, becoming, hoping, longing, etc.

What happened when you got annoyed? You just jumped off because you didn't want that. You didn't believe it meant something or there was something wrong with you, or that you had to be right. When we are annoyed, we want to be right. Needing to be right is suffering. Being wrong is fine, no problem.

Inquirer: *Yes, I did let it go.*

Sal: It's not even that you let it go, it's that there is just no desire in your mind to go in there. You know it is painful, so that desire doesn't appear. As long as the intention for truth is there, it just goes naturally by itself. There is no "I" to let it go, that would be another self: the self that is annoyed and the self that has to let it go. In truth, there was no desire in there that wants to be right or justified. The annoyance just came and went, and that is natural.

If you don't believe in ego, then where is it? Have a look. Have a holiday.

Inquirer: *Ego is floating around with all those thoughts.*

Sal: Ego is only the belief in separation. There is nothing floating around anywhere. If you stop believing it, then where is it? Not here, not anywhere. Look and see for yourself. Be clear about this. Have a holiday and see that your essential being, here and now, is free, and that, in truth, there is no ego floating around anywhere.

Ego is not a thing, it is just the belief that I am a separate object. And that belief comes and goes. If there is no ego, then what is there to fix? On the path, we are always purifying our mind, getting rid of our tendencies, practicing right behavior, etc. These are just things we were taught to do from ignorance.

What we are doing is the end of all beliefs—what happens after death, higher powers, the meaning of life, etc. Also, it's the end of the belief that some guru knows better than I do. How do I know that Ramana Maharshi knows better than I do? I can only believe it. How would I know, in fact? I only know what I know, and the only thing I know is, here and now, I am.

The only knowing is now, and now, I am aware, free. This is who I am. All of this philosophical knowing is nonsense, it can never be known in that way. Knowing that the Buddha is the great enlightened one is not knowing anything. It is simply a belief, right?

Inquirer: Right, because you could believe the same about Pat Robertson.

Sal: That's right, and many people do. During these eight weeks together, Sal was apparently the teacher and you were the inquirer, but who is who? Do I know something that you don't know? If you say yes, it's because of some nonsense programmed in your mind. What do I know that you don't know? I am not some guru, so wise and great and above you. I am just as ordinary as anyone else. I just have no problem with myself. I am fine as I am, and I don't need to figure out the meaning of life.

They say, "When you meet the Buddha along the path, kill him." No more gurus. They don't know a damn thing that you don't know for yourself now.

In truth, the only thing anyone can know, is now. That is the only real knowing. Knowing and aware are synonyms in my view.

⟨ೋ⟩

Nature of Truth

Inquirer: Truth is a big word.

Sal: When Pat Robertson (an Evangelical Christian preacher in America) states that Jesus is the only son of God, then yes, it is. Because he is making an empirical statement that can never be proven, it is just a belief. Truth has nothing to do with any kind of belief, it is simply now.

Obviously, now is true. Why deny that? It would just be silly. Now there is this knowing that is aware of whatever is appearing—this cup, this annoyance, this laughter, etc.

Other than now, all else is belief or fantasy, past and future. Not needing to know anything about life is freedom, a relief.

※

"Why" Questions

Inquirer: Why are we here?

Sal: I have no idea, are you a philosopher? If all of these great philosophers after thousands of years haven't answered that question, doesn't it mean that maybe there isn't an answer? Otherwise, it would be written in a book somewhere and we would all know.

We have no idea. There is no answer to why questions. "Why" is seeking; it is the carousel of philosophy. I have no idea and I don't care at all.

> **Inquirer:** *I do know that these ideas, like why am I here, are disruptive to the process of liberation.*

Sal: These ideas you have are self. The end of these ideas is the end of you, as self. This is freedom. So yes, you need to see that these ideas are ignorance, not wisdom. Once you see that they are ignorance, they are gone. Just like the belief in Santa Claus was gone when you found out it was ignorance.

Soul and Death

> **Inquirer:** *I read that the Buddha said don't worry if there is anything, like a soul, because you will know after liberation.*

Sal: Know, now. He didn't mean that once you become liberated, you will know what is going to happen after death. What is, is now. Is there anything behind the curtain of now?

> **Inquirer:** *No.*

Sal: Ok, that is why it takes great maturity for liberation because it means you don't know a thing about anything—future, after death, why, how, where did I come from, etc. It is a relief to be finished with all of that.

Liberation is the real maturity. It means I don't know anything, nor do I care. All I know is now—this is it. It is very stark. The only knowing is now. It's a relief, "Thank god I don't have to care or worry about what is going to happen, either after death or in the future, or why am I here." What a burden to feel the need to know that. Most people don't want to give up their beliefs or their false security that they are going to live forever. Not knowing is like being naked, here and now.

This takes time to resolve. Not that there is a goal, but in my own experience, and with almost everyone, it takes some time for this to become doubtless. How that works is by remaining authentic, recognizing what is true, and continually valuing what is true. See that the idea about a self continuing after death is just a belief, it is not a verifiable fact. I say, I don't know, and I don't care, because all I do know is here and now. If I believe an idea about after death, I am identifying with a self who desires immortality and who is becoming and seeking. You just see that, that's all.

All of the beliefs in an afterlife are just fairy tales for adults. It is a false sense of security, "I am going to live forever." These beliefs have no substance, they don't exist. Have a holiday, now. Is there anything behind the curtain of now? Where are these beliefs, now? They are just insubstantial thoughts that appear and disappear. Be finished with all of that. A belief may come up again, and then it is going to be gone.

I don't remember a moment when it was finished; I just noticed more in hindsight, "Oh, it's over." There is no goal, but do stay authentic and be mature. Be reconciled with the fact that, it is not that you don't want to know anything, it is that you actually don't know anything about all of that. Whatever you think you know has to be a belief since you have no proof. You do not know what is going to happen when this body drops, so just be finished with all of that. Since you don't and can't know, why bother?

This false sense of security, having a belief about what is going to happen after death, is not real security. The only real security is not knowing. We think our beliefs are security, but that is not true. Not knowing is the true security because that doesn't change does it?

> **Inquirer:** No, that doesn't change, and it doesn't limit.

Sal: Right, it doesn't limit. Now, when you have a holiday, isn't it the same as when you came out of the womb? No head, just aware, knowing, no data in the brain. Look, right now; don't think about past, or subconscious, or anything. Here now, is there any data? Have a holiday and see this.

༄

Inquirer: *No, there isn't.*

Sal: That's right, there isn't. There is nothing. When you came out of the womb, there was no data. And right now, there is no data, so what is the difference? See for yourself if your essential being is the same now as when you came out of the womb.

༄

When a belief like that appears and you identify with it, then, in that moment, you are that belief. When that belief goes, you go.

༄

INQUIRY SEVEN — BEING FINISHED

Coming to know what is true about your essential being takes maturity. Most people are not ready to stop buying into their dearly and fearfully held grasp on self which is just the amalgamation of impressions that have been recorded in their minds by culture, society, family and religion. Most of us hold on to the "known," the ever-changing data (all of the experiences, stories, beliefs, hopes, feelings of inferiority or superiority, the need to be special, cynicism about awakening, etc.), as a means of security with great fear of losing "myself." For most, it seems like a lot to lose, for it will leave them with nothing to hold on to as a "me."

But the security of the known is fickle. Why? Because it is in constant change, decay and death. The only true security is in valuing your essential being because this is always true and never changes. So, there can be no fear of losing it, and hence, no insecurity. Being ready to bypass all of that fear and grasping long enough to come to know what is true is not possible for most people.

It takes maturity and readiness for that. Usually, it is the result of being tired of seeking in the world of form and spirituality and then seeing, for oneself, that no lasting satisfaction is found in either of them. Also, it happens because someone is completely exhausted with suffering.

It takes a far greater maturity to be finished. Being finished means seeking is over. It means you have come to know what is true—who you are is free, you lack nothing and are whole and complete already, and there is nothing greater to attain in the future. It means you are reconciled that what is, is. It is doubtless and irreversible.

For this to happen, one has to have a genuine desire for freedom, really see the value of truth and value that at all times. If we take for granted what we have come to know and allow the tendency (it is only a tendency) of seeking for something more to continue, by reading more books and looking at more teachers, we will just be right back on the carousel of mind. And again, we will be lost in the belief of an inadequate, or grandiose, self.

If you have truly come to know your essential being, you see for yourself that it is doubtless already and there is no greater enlightenment to attain in the future. Ordinary, simple and completely obvious—I am now, and have always been, free.

Any ideas of a greater enlightenment must be seen as only that, more ideas and more beliefs. We get them from books, teachers, culture, religion, etc., and they commonly revolve around attaining higher states, feeling a certain way, or being in bliss every second of every day.

Don't believe it for a second. You know who you are. Don't fall for that trap. Be simple. Value truth above all else. It is liberation already. See this, know this and know its value. There is no goal to attain like, "I will be liberated in the future." Right here, right now, liberation is. See and know this for yourself and be finished.

Recognize that it is already the end. Don't project that tomorrow you will have some doubts, or maybe something will appear that will throw you off, cause you to get lost, or identify with self. See, NOW. Here and now, recognize that you are aware, free, and that it is your essential being, now and always. See that it is finished, NOW.

What we are doing here is coming to the end of seeking and becoming. You are what you are, which is aware, free. And, this body/mind organism, is appearing in aware, right now. This is who you are. What you are not is your personal history or future aspirations. These are fantasies because they are not actual, now.

So then, why argue with what is? If something doesn't feel so great, it is what it is. Arguing with it by trying to change it or get rid of it just causes unnecessary suffering. Wave is ocean. Right now, if the wave doesn't feel so good, it is still ocean. Then it vanishes and is gone forever, never to appear again. Only memory tells you that it still exists. This creates suffering, now, for something that is not even actual.

You are ocean, the absolute, all-inclusive, free, and you are the limited wave that is appearing, now. You are not the wave that appeared two days ago, or even two seconds ago. Those waves are gone forever. So, why hold on to them, and give them value and meaning, and let them affect you, now? You are also not any wave that may appear in the future, like the enlightened wave for example. Why hope and pray and compare yourself now with an ideal of who you will become in the future? That is pure fantasy and simply not true.

We are talking about the end of seeking, the end of being anything other than what you are, which is free—free to feel good and free to feel bad. Free to be whatever is appearing now, without it making you believe that something is wrong with you, that you lack something, that you are not complete or fulfilled, or that you are not enlightened. You are free as this body, free as aware, free-flowing, everything appearing and dissolving, here and now.

The Fan Analogy

We are not trying to change anything. We are just coming to see what is true and how we are operating. We see that our essential being is free, and that self is simply a temporary appearance based on belief in the amalgamation of thoughts and experiences recorded in this brain. We also see that self comes and goes like any other experience, and that there is nothing to transcend. This is the end of seeking and becoming. When it is completely doubtless, it is permanent. For now, some doubts may appear, but when it is not possible for a doubt to appear, it is irreversible. Just as you can never believe there is a Santa Claus again.

Ramana Maharshi speaks of the fan analogy. He says that when you turn the power switch off, the fan starts to slow down. The blades of these ceiling fans are very big, so it takes a while for them to stop. If you turn the switch back on, the fan starts to speed up again. Eventually, if the switch is kept off, the fan stops.

What is the "on" switch? Belief. You have believed your whole life that you are separate, the doer, and that something is inherently wrong with you. When you have a holiday, the switch is turned off. Then maybe a doubt will appear, which is simply a belief. Have another holiday, and you see again what is true—I lack nothing and am complete already, free already. Then the switch is off. That doesn't mean that you can never focus on anything—work and even thoughts that need to be attended to. That is a perfectly natural function of attention.

Eventually, with continuing to see what is true, it will not be possible to believe anymore that these things indicate anything—you are not free, or something is wrong with you. Then the belief switch is off, permanently—thoughts, no thoughts, pain, pleasure, etc. It doesn't matter. It is finished. How that happens is by valuing what is true, and not valuing the ever-changing content of mind. This is not something you "do." It just happens when you are ready and have come to know something other than what you have believed.

Worship

You have heard about worshipping the divine or the guru. But the true worship is valuing what is true. It is not worship of the other, or of some beliefs. This is immature.

In Bhakti Yoga, the path of devotion, you worship god or the guru. But the true Bhakti is the same as Jnana, the path of knowing, which is what we do together here. True Bhakti is to stay true to truth, and Jnana is also to come to know and stay true to truth.

So yes, be a real Bhakta, value what is true—value your essential being. This, by itself, is what resolves all your doubts. See, without judgment, that when a belief appears, it's not a problem. Know it is only a belief and be done. It is the end of arguing with what is, of thinking I am the great knower, and of needing to be right.

As the Bible says, "Worship no false idols above me." The idol we worship above all else is self/ego. We spend our whole life worshipping me, my, etc. Now that you have come to know something different and seen its value, worship this truth, above self.

How do you want to live: free, or in this painful limiting worship of self?

Getting Real

If you find yourself going into stories (which can happen for anyone), going over and over and trying to resolve or understand them, or trying to find some meaning in there, etc., just know something. In that moment, that is what you want, to get in there. There is a belief that it means something, that it has some value. This is not to judge yourself, it is just to see what is true. In that moment, that is what you want. Because if you want freedom, well, here it is. If you find yourself doing that, then get real, see what is true and jump off.

The Path and the Goal are the Same

Take time each day, when you are not busy, to have holidays, while sitting around the house or taking a walk. A holiday is the recognition that, here and now, your essential being, you, are free. The goal is already attained, and you see this in a holiday. A holiday is both the path and the goal. It is a means of recognizing what is true already, and also, a means of allowing doubts to resolve completely.

The End

All that is needed is to be reconciled with the simple fact that all there is, is now. If that is truly reckoned with, then what further is there to attain or transcend? Whatever is appearing is appearing. I say, this is the end of seeking, the natural human condition, free from becoming anything other than what is, now.

For most people, that is not acceptable. But it can't be denied—the truth is that all there is, is now, and whatever is now, is now. To argue with that is pointless. Any ideas we have that there will be some more transcendence, that something is going to click, or that the enlightened condition is going to appear, are just ideas. See this!

These ideas have just been impressed in the mind from all the books we have read and all the teachers we have heard. One of the great crimes of humanity is the idea of heaven or nirvana after you die, or enlightenment in the future. These ideas have created a world of dissatisfaction with what is now. Liberation is a full reckoning with what is now. There is nothing more. We have come to believe that we are going to make something of ourselves on some level in the future. Clearly, this is what we have been taught. When we came out of the womb, that was not in operation at all.

Stay off the carousels—psychological, philosophical and spiritual. But you can't do that until you've recognized them for what they are, fantasy. When the time is right, you stop because you have seen the fallacy of it and have come to know something different. There is nothing to become other than what is. To argue with what is now is immature. What is, is. This is truth.

PART 2

PART TWO — ADDITIONAL QUESTIONS AND ANSWERS

Trust

Inquirer: *I trust you, I trust what you say.*

Sal: Don't trust what I say, see if it's true. I don't want anyone to trust me or believe me. I want you to see if it's true. Now that you've seen for yourself that what I've said is true, you trust me. But it's not because of me. It's because of you. You've seen what is true.

Trust truth. Don't trust Sal. Your own knowing is the real guru. I am not your guru; your own knowing is.

⌘

They say the real guru is within you, don't they? We don't understand, and we don't know what it means. It just means the guru is your own knowing, truth. Trust that guru, that's the only guru you need to trust.

Inquirer: *Thank you for making that clear, finally.*

❧

Does it Take Time to be Finished?

Inquirer: *Does it take a while to not fall into stories anymore, daydreaming, etc.?*

Sal: We're not trying to change the mind; we are just losing the belief that there is something of value in there, or that there is a doer, etc. Beliefs are being eradicated. Thoughts will still appear, no problem. Thoughts appear for me too, and sometimes I attend to them, even if they are not important. It doesn't make me think I am unenlightened.

Inquirer: *Do I need to constantly remember that I am aware and free?*

Sal: I don't walk around having to know who I am; it is finished. I know who I am. You don't walk around knowing there is no Santa Claus, do you? You just know. You don't have to look under the chimney to make sure. You are not going to forget.

Inquirer: *I can always look and see, right?*

Sal: Yes, of course, for now, until it is completely doubtless. Then you never need to notice again. It is just known, like there is no Santa Claus. If there are thoughts you are attending to, no problem. You are still fully aware, just aware of thoughts in that moment. There is focused attention, completely natural, and there is unfocused attention, also completely natural. In both, you are free.

Just be natural. We are just coming to be finished with thinking there should be something different than what is— "I have to be more enlightened, in a state of awareness, have no thoughts, or be in bliss..." Who said all of that nonsense anyway?

> **Inquirer:** *I wonder about being in the presence of people who also recognize this.*

Sal: I understand. I am not around anyone else that knows this. I know maybe a few people in the world who do. Most people I know are very esoteric, mystical, even religious. They are not at all interested in this. What you are saying is nice, to be amongst people who know this. But first of all, there are very few people who do. Secondly, the sanghas (spiritual communities) and ashrams always turn into a dogmatic gathering or a religion. You don't need that. You can be around anyone, it doesn't matter.

I'd much rather talk to a regular person than a spiritual seeker of enlightenment, espousing their philosophies and talking about how great their guru is. I'd rather talk to a carpenter, really.

You are alone in this, and even your husband, boyfriend, lover or friend doesn't need to know this, it doesn't matter.

> **Inquirer:** *How do you see others who may not know this?*

Sal: I see that I am not inferior or superior to anyone at all. I'm not inferior to the Buddha, and I am not superior to the Evangelical Christian. We are all the same; maybe some know something that others may not. I know there is no doer here, and there is no doer anywhere. That is true whether the other person knows it or not.

As we have seen, we can take no credit for this shift happening here, nor can we assign blame that it may not have happened elsewhere. If someone wants to tell me about their esoteric ideas, since I know that is just the way they are, I let them do it. I would never try to convince them of anything. That would be arrogance.

When Douglas Harding said, "Can't you see, I'm just space for you to be," he meant everyone, not just others who have had this shift. You don't need the other to confirm you or be supportive, you know who you are, finished. As you said, you can't forget, you know.

❧

Conditioning

> **Inquirer:** *I'm sure you understand that it's not so much an angst, but a deep, pervasive hunger.*

Sal: What are you hungering for?

> **Inquirer:** *Is that a trick question?*

Sal: Yes.

> **Inquirer:** *Got it. The hunger comes from a sense of seeking.*

Sal: Yes. To paraphrase U.G. Krishnamurti, when that hunger goes, you go. When you reckon with the fact that there is no independent, empirical, long-standing self in there, the seeking goes. That is what seeing there is no doer is about. Who would hunger? It must just be some idea, some thought programmed in by culture, the impressions you have collected and taken for granted?

Inquirer: Then there is just sensation arising without the urge to give it a name and identify with it.

Sal: The urge to find "something" is just a tendency impressed in your mind. There is no "you" in there who is hungering. There is just the belief that something is fundamentally wrong or missing. When that belief goes, it's over, there is nothing more to attain other than what you are, right now. That last sentence is the end when fully reckoned with. Can you see that?

Inquirer: Yes, absolutely.

Sal: Good, then get real. Jump off the carousels of mind. Stop figuring it all out. Know nothing. That is what a holiday shows.

This reliance on needing to know something is bondage. Knowing nothing and needing to know nothing about life is it! You're just falling for your old games. Stop, get real. Here and now, what is, is. It can't be denied. There is nothing more than what is, now.

Inquirer: The impressions are seductive and deeply ingrained to trigger the philosophical notions that spew out, the need to be in control of "destiny," etc.

Sal: The impressions are nothing if you are ready to be done. Don't give them any power. They have no power other than what you give them, so don't. By that I mean, get real, jump off, know nothing.

Inquirer: I find there is a blind spot to their arising—as if I remain unaware or ignorant to the mirage.

Sal: Have a holiday now, and tell me where they are hiding.

Inquirer: They are nowhere.

Sal: That's right. The blind spot is your belief in them, that they mean something. It is just the belief that has to go, that's all, not the impressions. A lifetime of being very intelligent and intellectual takes a bit of time, no problem. It was the same for me. You have been relying on the structure of thought as the knowing function your whole life. This is a different way.

Inquirer: On the one hand, there is this thing we refer to as the conditioning. There is what we point to with the words, "get real." The conflict arises as we identify with the conditioning as being who we are, the doer who exists as an independent separate entity with choice. More accurately, the conditioning appears to exist.

Sal: I don't see any conditioning. That is for seekers who want to get purity and attain enlightenment. I only see here and now. And for you, who wants to be free, I have to say, be honest and see that conditioning doesn't exist, in truth. I say that so you will lose the belief in that and stop giving it power.

⚜

Is There Only Now?

Inquirer: There is only now, I know that.

Sal: Is there any past, empirically? Or future, empirically?

Inquirer: No.

Sal: The only truth is now. If there's only now, was any of this created in the past?

Inquirer: No, there's only now, there's no future and there's no past.

Sal: Whatever there is now, is just now, it didn't come from anywhere because where would it come from? Some past that doesn't exist? This is a very stark realization, that whatever is appearing now didn't come from anywhere, it's just appearing, now. The Big Bang is now.

There is no past and no future, so whatever is appearing now is just appearing and dissolving, simultaneously, now. And if that's true, then all the philosophical questions like, "Where did I come from?" and "Why am I here?" are removed. They mean nothing.

Inquirer: That's all keeping us from the now.

Sal: That's all keeping us in the belief that self and time are empirically truth. Self and time are codependent. Self doesn't exist without time, does it? Self needs time to exist.

Inquirer: Yes, and that creates all the duality.

Sal: So, get real. Not that you can do that, but give it up. Not that you can do that either, but get real. Give it up. Recognize what's true, see for yourself.

Inquirer: The roots are pulling me in.

Sal: Don't give them so much power by saying that. They're just some thoughts passing by, that's it. It's just data programmed into your head. There is no power to them at all. If you say they pull you in, you give them power and, "Poor me, they're so strong, I can't win." This is giving them power. In truth, they're not pulling you in because there is no "you" to be pulled in, they're just passing.

Have a holiday, now. See this.

⚜

Why am I Here?

Inquirer: I'd like to know why you think we're here.

Sal: I have no idea. I am not a philosopher, and it doesn't interest me. I couldn't care less.

No one else knows either. Otherwise, we would know by now. With all the great philosophers we've had since Aristotle and Plato, no one has come up with an answer. Don't you think someone would know by now? Asking why we're here is a philosophical question.

Liberation has nothing to do with philosophy, which is of the mind. Questions like, "I am confused," "I don't know what's true," "I have all these ideas about soul and death," "Why am I here?", come because of the data in this brain. We're confused, not knowing what's true, who I am. We suffer and then want to know why am I here. What's the point of it all. These are just ideas.

Inquirer: *I think we're here to get out of here, that's what I think.*

Sal: That's another philosophy. I have no idea of anything. I leave that to the philosophers. Ten thousand years from now we'll have this meeting and see if they have come up with the answer. I guarantee they won't. Why not? Because there is no why. What is, is. Is there some past or future? Have a holiday.

Look, right now. You can answer this question yourself, now. And if you do, answer it once and for all. In truth, is there a past or future? Anything behind the curtain?

Inquirer: *No.*

Sal: What is, is. Is that true? The only truth is now.

Inquirer: *It's all there is.*

Sal: Now ask why? Why is this as it is? You see, it is a moot point. What is, simply is. "Why" will keep you seeking forever.

What is, is now, it doesn't care why. There is no possible way of knowing. There is no why, there is only now and what is. Why? I have no idea. Where did this come from? I have no idea. In fact, I say it came from nowhere, it just is.

The question "why" just appears, and in that moment, you are that question. Believing there is a "you" that came up with the question is self, it's ego. But see it's impersonal because there's no "you" that came up with that question, "why?" It was just programmed into your head. Are you in there inventing the question, "Why am I here?" or does the question just appear?

> **Inquirer:** *It appears. It's still floating around my space. I recognize it, yes, I see.*

Sal: You just see again and again that whatever appears, here and now, is just as it is. Did you create this moment? Look, now.

> **Inquirer:** *No, it's here.*

Sal: Whatever thoughts are appearing now, did you create them or are they just appearing, now?

Inquirer: *They're just appearing, now.*

Sal: It's not even that you didn't create them. It's that there is no "you" to create anything. As long as you think you are the chooser, you will think there's a choice in that. I say there is no choice. You can say, "Well this choice was made," but I say that in truth, there is no choice. What is, is. There's no choice because if there's choice, there's someone choosing, and I say that's not true. So, there is no chooser, and there is no choice either. There is no free will either.

Inquirer: *So, you can go with the flow.*

Sal: You are the flow.

Inquirer: *Okay, yes.*

Sal: The way to reconcile this and reckon with it is to see if it's true or not. Not to believe it's true. Believing it's true is just another philosophy, it doesn't mean anything for freedom. Tell me, where are you, show me. Show me this one who is choosing. Find this one who is choosing.

You see why it takes a great maturity to give all this stuff up. Not that you give it up, but to see what's true, and to be finished. It can take time, no problem. Have holidays and see again if what I am saying is true or not. Because if what I am saying is not true, then you'll see. But if it's true, you will also see. Know what's true and truth will set you free. It's not: "Give up beliefs and that will set you free," or, "Experience something and that will set you free." You just know what's true.

Why is there this belief that there is a "why"? Because it has been programmed into your head. It wasn't there when you came out of the womb, this information, or any of it. Why do you think there is a soul? Because this information was put into your head and so you believe that there's a soul here. Is this true? Or am I making it up?

> **Inquirer:** *It's totally true, yes.*

Sal: Arguing means, "I need to understand why and figure it out." This is arguing with what is.

> **Inquirer:** *I liked the thing you said about you are the "why" or the "why" is you.*

Sal: The "why" question appears. When that goes, you go.

In this moment, a holiday happens, and you see there is no self. Then, in the next moment, "Why am I here?" appears and you are appearing as, "Why am I here?" That's who you are appearing as in that moment. Then that question passes and once again, you recognize that the natural default human condition is free. And then, "What's the meaning of life?" appears and, in that moment, you are appearing as the question, "What's the meaning of life?" You are not someone who is having the question, but the question itself.

Inquirer: Right, that's who you are in that moment, yes.

Sal: There is the question, "Why am I here?" and then you think there is someone else in here having that question. But I say, there isn't. If you think there is, that's just another thought appearing. "I am having this question," and "What's the answer to this question?" are just more thoughts. When that stops, then you don't flow with life, you are the flow of life.

Inquirer: Yes.

Sal: This takes a great maturity, because it's jumping off these stupid things.

Emotions

> **Inquirer:** *I've noticed I have an emotional evenness to every day. There's no big highs, no big lows.*

Sal: That can change. There will be big highs and lows emotionally. Things happen, for me too.

Inquirer: I understand that's not a goal, but this evenness has been more prevalent in my life over the past year than ever before. That reactive element is not glowing as hot as it used to. It doesn't mean that I don't laugh, or I don't get excited. I'm not a zombie.

Sal: We're just coming to the end of seeking and becoming here. What is, is. There could be a strong emotion, no problem. We're not seeking anything other than what is. We're not going into the past rummaging around our subconscious to explain what caused this or caused that. What is, is. Again, it's very stark.

It's not a state of equanimity where nothing perturbs us because this body/mind organism does get perturbed. When someone dies, it gets perturbed. A baby is born, it gets happy. A truck runs over the foot, it gets pain. This body/mind is going to be touched, always.

The idea we have of Buddha or Ramana Maharshi sitting in a loincloth up on a rock somewhere is not how we live. You live in the regular world. In the midst of the world, where you live is family, kids, work, all this stuff going on; the body/mind definitely has experiences. Emotions and thoughts are experiences this body/mind has. We're not trying to get into a state where we're Buddha-like in the midst of an emotion. That's not what I speak about. We're just finished arguing with whatever is. Feels good, feels bad. Ok, that's what it is.

The spiritual carrot that you will be equanimous and never have any bad experiences and always be in bliss does such a disservice. That's such nonsense. We get these ideas through reading and listening to teachers. We paint a picture in our mind, we see a teacher, a guru sitting there, and we project our beliefs that this person is always in bliss. We project that we're such a loser because we're not always in bliss. I don't buy it. There's only now. You are only who you are. That's it. There is no other alternative.

> **Inquirer:** *I know thought is rational in the way it operates when I am doing a task and I am learning how to cook something or put something together. That seems to be its place. Often, it runs incessantly. So, it would be nice if it was quiet in times when it's not needed.*

Sal: It does get quiet in that way, in the way of not trying to change what is or become something else. But let's face it, if something unpleasant happens in the day, the mind records that impression and then it replays that impression as thoughts. That's the mechanical functioning.

> *Inquirer: Okay, so negative/positive again seems to be just another form of interpretation. What happens, happens. Then I think, "It is not good for me to be negative." I lost money on this deal. That is bad. Then I chew over it again and again.*

Sal: If I invested money and it was lost, that's not so good. I'm not going to say it's good. I would prefer to have made money, but the story I tell over and over is the suffering. This can go.

> *Inquirer: Right, and then it puts a cloud over the day. Then you start to think about how maybe you're not as sharp as you were, your security now is threatened. It snowballs.*

Sal: Of course, that often happens. That can go. In that way, the mind can be quiet. Thoughts are still going to be going on. That's the job of the mind. It records impressions and replays them as thoughts. That's just mechanical.

Inquirer: But then when the mind replays it as thought, it goes through a filter that is influenced greatly by this desire to become more.

Sal: Yes, and after we no longer believe in a discrete self entity, which can happen, then the thoughts just play themselves out like an old radio in the background, for the most part.

Inquirer: They don't have that emotional hook.

Sal: They can be of an emotional nature, but they may not be able to hook you into the story and turn that ripple into a wave and then into a tsunami. Thoughts can have an emotional flavor, of course. Something not so pleasant happens, and then thoughts can be emotionally not so pleasant. Thoughts and emotions are completely linked. They're not separate.

That's natural as well. They can be just playing in the background and passing quickly. Some people, however, hold on to the same story their whole life. It's sad, you know, but true, isn't it? Those stories stay on forever.

Life in the world that we live in, amongst people, family, friends and work, is challenging. That's just the way it is. Life, when I live in India, is very simple. Very little challenge. It's nice. Here, in the West, where we live with all of this stuff, this body/mind organism is going to have things going on. The experiencing entity, this body/mind organism, experiences. It's not meant to experience only pleasant things. That's not its nature. It's built to experience both pleasant and unpleasant. That won't change, but that's what we want. We want it to only experience the pleasant, that's the fantasy and it's not realistic.

☙❧

Feeling Things More Intensely Than Before

Inquirer: *It seems that after this work I feel things more intensely than I did before. Like when something unpleasant happens, I seem to feel it more strongly.*

Sal: Normally, what we all do is try to not feel unpleasant experiences. So, we do things like avoiding, masking with drugs or alcohol, distracting ourselves with some activity, or simply denying what we are feeling. We do anything possible to not feel bad. And, when we are on the spiritual path, we come to believe that it is possible to achieve a new state of consciousness where we will never experience anything unpleasant or painful, especially emotionally.

What spiritual seekers do is feel or think that this negative emotion is an indication that there is something wrong, they are not enlightened or something like that. This adds on to the emotion by creating an additional problem—a belief that the emotion is "wrong."

When a child has an emotion and feels bad, it just feels bad, period. It is not questioning whether or not that emotion means something or is wrong. And a moment later they are laughing again. If we have the attitude that the negative emotion is wrong, we will feel that we are failing at our spiritual goal for feeling bad, or we will deny that we feel bad to others and ourselves.

Now you have come to know something different. First of all, your essential being is aware and free already. There is nothing you need to change or attain for that to be true; you simply need to recognize it. Secondly, you come to see that you are not the doer, chooser or creator, and that whatever is appearing simply is as it is. When this is truly recognized and reconciled, then the movement to change what is doesn't arise. Neither does the movement to avoid, deny, mask or replace what is.

When this stops, then whatever is arising as a feeling/emotion has free reign to be there and be fully experienced. This may then feel more intense than when you were avoiding, masking, etc. But, when you do stop with all of those strategies of avoidance and control, these feelings/emotions appear and flow by very naturally. Usually, much quicker than they would if you were employing strategies of avoidance. Why? Because in using those strategies, you are empowering those emotions with the belief that they are very important, have great value, and have the ability to affect your well-being in the long run. Feeding them this energy propagates them, does not allow them to flow on by naturally, and keeps you suffering much longer than is needed.

Continue to value what you have come to know—you lack nothing, are complete and whole already, and are free and unbound. Nothing is excluded in who you are, and emotions are a very natural aspect of this human form. There is nothing wrong with you if you feel something strongly. So, why deny that? Just value your essential free nature and see that all things flow by naturally.

⁂

Emotions are Natural

> **Inquirer:** *I can understand if somebody sticks a pin in me, or if I put my hand over the fire, I react,*

and I pull it away. Then the pain goes away. But emotionally speaking, I'm saying to the degree that I'm hanging on to past impressions... it is to that degree that there will be some sort of an angst or clinging, or commentary.

Sal: The body is designed with nerves so that when a pin goes in your hand it hurts and you react. The body is designed to have emotional responses as well. If something happens that's painful, the body is going to feel it in that moment. In the moment of loss, the body will experience some fear or sadness. The body functions in that way.

Inquirer: This is what I don't think I understand. The emotion is a tendency from an impression that I have...

Sal: Well, no it's not.

Inquirer: So, you're saying there's emotion separate from conditioning?

Sal: Yes. Thought is very natural, right? Thought appears naturally, doesn't it? The brain's function is to record impressions and replay them as thoughts. That's natural isn't it? Well, emotions are just as natural as well.

I want to be clear about this. If the body gets cut, there's a physical pain. Likewise, the brain records impressions and replays them as thoughts. So far, these are natural, right? But you're telling me that emotions are not natural. That means there's something unenlightened about you because there are emotions. If this body wasn't naturally inclined to have emotions, it wouldn't, would it? Emotions are natural.

If something so-called negative or unpleasant happens in your circumstances, thoughts can come, and emotions can come. This is natural. This is not the creation of a self. The self is when you then make a story out of these emotions, the "poor me" story. And you get in there and turn it around into a big thing. That's suffering right there. If someone I care about deeply dies, am I not supposed to feel something? I'm sorry. It's ridiculous.

> **Inquirer:** *How come when a tree dies, or I see a dead squirrel on the road that got in the way of another car, I don't feel so bad?*

Sal: It's not your child; you are not emotionally connected to those things. In that sense, you could say that's personal with your child. It's natural. Are we trying to become some kind of robot? I'm not going to argue if someone I love dies and I feel some sadness. But I'll tell you, it would probably pass pretty quickly. I'm not going to mope for weeks, months, and years. There could be a strong emotion appearing. It's natural.

Inquirer: This is an example of vanity trying to figure out what the future's going to look like. The truth is that I don't know how I will behave in any situation.

Sal: That's very true what you just said. It's also the projection of what you think the enlightened person is like, that she is going to be unattached and have no emotions. I'm sorry. I don't buy it. I see emotions appear here, and I don't argue with them. That's truth. I don't try to get rid of them, and I don't go into them, so they don't propagate. I don't keep the belief switch on, so the fan keeps spinning forever. I don't try to avoid them, believe them, or propagate them in any way. The emotion is going to appear, and the emotion is going to disappear, just like a wave.

⌘

Anxiety

> **Inquirer:** *Yesterday, I had a lot of anxiety. So, I took a holiday in the middle of it. I saw that it doesn't matter what is happening, that nothing can touch who I am, which is freedom. I just feel*

that here is this broken thing, even though who I
am is unbound. I see that I am free, but the body
is not. I just don't see it as all-inclusive for some
reason.

Sal: There are a few things to say. First of all, are you not this body? There are teachings that I say are halfway around the circle, which say, "I am awareness and this form is not who I am, so it doesn't matter what happens to this body and in this world." This is an extreme view, but I know people who have this view. It is not the truth. The truth is I am this body as well. I am not what I thought—only this body, so limited and separate. Aware includes everything, including this body, including anxiety, anger, or whatever is appearing.

You say that you know you are free, but the body is not free. Well, if you want to look at it that way then the body is never free, it is what experiences. It is also free because it is free to experience whatever it experiences without a self in here to argue with it. What we are taught is to believe that there is something wrong with us because anger is appearing— "I am obviously unenlightened when anger appears." Who said that? If anger is appearing, it is true. There is only now.

I say that liberation is knowing that what is, is, and the end of arguing with it or thinking I am wrong because some anger is appearing. The truth is, there is anger. You didn't create it. What we do is one of two things—we either get into the story of anger, what this person did, and then this wave of anger turns into a big tsunami of anger, or we get into self-blame, "I am so unenlightened because I am angry." Either way, the wave of anger, which comes naturally, is not allowed to go naturally.

I say there is nothing wrong with you. You can stop arguing with what is. Aren't these emotions natural?

> **Inquirer:** *I guess if I could control them I would be equanimous.*

Sal: That is what we think—we can control them. But what we are really doing is creating another self. The self that is angry, and the self that needs to control the anger and be equanimous— "I am the great controller in here who is going to be equanimous." That is just ego, isn't it? The one who is remaining equanimous is ego.

A wave in the ocean comes out of nowhere, and then it goes, unless there is the idea that you need to do something about it. When a wave appears, isn't it still ocean? It comes from nowhere, it appears and then disappears, never to be seen again. It's just gone. When anger appears, in the moment of anger, you are appearing as anger. Then that subsides, and you are appearing as happiness. If anger appears again, it is not even the same anger. You are never ever appearing the same twice.

Liberation is a couple of things. One aspect of liberation is being finished seeking and becoming—more equanimous, more spiritual, more enlightened, more popular, acclaimed or whatever. Another aspect is knowing that whatever is, is. It is the end of arguing with what is and thinking it is wrong. Why? Because whatever is appearing now must be true. What is not true is the idea that I should be equanimous. It's a lie because I am not being equanimous.

Coming to the end of seeking and being fully reconciled that what is, is, is the true equanimity. It is the peace that passes understanding. If, for example, you feel something for someone who is suffering, it won't feel good, it won't feel like peace. The peace is, "Ok, this is what is, no problem."

We are not trying to transcend our humanity here. Be fully human with the knowing, I am as I am, and all is good with me.

This body/mind organism is the experiencing entity. It will always experience something, and it is not always going to be pleasant. Why would it be? We have an idea that enlightenment means I am always going to experience bliss, or something like that. Who says this? This is simply not natural.

❧

Dealing With Negative Appearances

Inquirer: It's amazing the amount of stuff that's swirling around in our lives, but sometimes it seems very personal, like what's going on with me right now.

Sal: Let's look into this a little bit because it is important and it's also very valuable. If you're in a meditation retreat for a month and you're in peace and bliss, you feel great. You get out of the meditation retreat, your mind is so clear, and you think, "Oh my God, I'm so enlightened." Then a month later, your business falls apart, or your shoulder hurts, or your boyfriend dumps you and then this body/mind gets thrown into a big conundrum. It's completely natural. Why wouldn't it? This body/mind is the experiencing entity, it doesn't only experience pleasant and peaceful things, it also experiences negative things, painful things, confusing things. It will always be that way.

In the meditation retreat, you feel so happy and blissful and then a month later, all this stuff happens, and you think: "Oh my God, what happened to my enlightenment?" Now there are a lot of thoughts and fears going on, so I must not be enlightened anymore. But you can consider these things grace. In the midst of all these things, look, you're still free. That's what a holiday is about. In the midst of these things, just notice, not for long, not to try to resolve it, change it, or get rid of it. But just, in the midst of it, a holiday shows you once again that in truth, "I am free." If, in the midst of all these difficult appearances, you can recognize that you're free, then it will become doubtless.

Liberation points to "whatever is, is." It's the full reckoning with this, that whatever is, is, and it's the end of arguing with whatever is, or thinking that there's something wrong with me because there's something negative appearing. Liberation means, "I am finished, I know I am free."

There is only now. Is this true? If in fact there's only now, then whatever is appearing now, is true, including negative things. If it's shoulder pain, it's true because it's appearing now. If it's concern because your business is falling apart and there is fear, worry, or sadness appearing, then this is what is. But, if on the other hand, there is the thought, "Oh no, there is that appearing, therefore I must not be enlightened, I have to be more enlightened in the future," that's a fantasy isn't it? That's not true. Why is it not true? Because what's true is that there is some sadness because the business is falling apart.

This body/mind goes through whatever it is going to go through. Sometimes life is easy and sometimes it's very challenging. To expect that it is going to be anything different than that, and things are going to be smooth sailing all the time is not realistic. That is just more becoming and is not what we're doing here.

We're coming to see that I am free, no matter what. This is the peace that passes understanding. It's not bliss, happiness or feeling good all the time. The peace that passes understanding is the end of arguing with what is. Because on top of this business problem that is causing concern, we add other things too: "I shouldn't be having these feelings." We make the story spin out in many more directions than it needs to. And then the original mental appearance doesn't flow by naturally.

❦

Equanimity

Inquirer: *I'd like to discuss equanimity, you know, if something good happens or something* *bad happens, you just say, "Okay, it doesn't matter." One thing isn't better than the other. One of the things I believe is involved with liberation, or maybe it's even liberation itself, is the thing where you don't become mentally and emotionally unbalanced when something super great happens or when something super bad happens. Is equanimity a result of liberation or is that something that occurs?*

Sal: Did I say the word equanimity or say you should be equanimous?

> **Inquirer:** *No. When you were talking about the value of emotional and mental health, and the fact that you're not thrown off kilter when something good or bad happens, I thought you were referring to equanimity.*

Sal: No, because equanimity implies two. For example, there is a "me" that is equanimous in the midst of the appearance of anger. Equanimity is a teaching on the path that says you should remain equanimous no matter what's appearing. That's not exactly what I am speaking about though.

In the moment, when an appearance of anger is here, this self is anger. Self/ego is an appearance, it comes and goes; there's no empirical self that has been here your whole life. A hundred times a day you default to the natural human condition, which is free and not focused. But then something happens, and anger appears. In that moment, that is what self looks like; self is appearing as anger, right?

Then the anger subsides and again your default condition is free. Then the next moment self appears as happiness or whatever it might be. During the appearance of anger, there is not someone else here to be equanimous, is there? In the moment of anger, that's who you are appearing as, anger.

It's like the ocean. In the moment of a wave, ocean is appearing as wave, and then that wave is gone, never to return again. The self doesn't come back as the same wave. Another wave appears but it's a completely different wave, and in that moment, ocean is appearing as the wave of anger, and then that's gone. During that time, ocean is still here, and ocean is always equanimous. You don't have to try to have equanimity; that would mean there would be another self there that's trying to remain equanimous. There would be the self which is anger and the self that's trying to remain equanimous. This doesn't really get to the point of what I'm speaking about. And it's good to be finished with that teaching of equanimity.

If the phone company overcharged me, and I am on the phone yelling at them because I am angry, I am not equanimous. I am yelling. I am not going be equanimous if someone is killing my dog.

This knowing is final. I know that I am free, and even in the midst of anger, I am still free, just anger is appearing. I don't think I am so unenlightened because anger is appearing, and I am not remaining equanimous.

Inquirer: *I do think that, yes.*

Sal: That's right, that's because you've been taught to believe that if anger appears...

Inquirer: *I failed...*

Sal: Yes, I failed, and I was supposed to remain equanimous. You see, this is not a helpful teaching. Maybe it helps somewhere along the path for people to see something differently, but not for what you're doing now, because now you're finished. What we're doing is coming to know what's true, finally, finished. Whatever appears, appears, and whatever disappears, disappears. That's it—anger, happiness, sadness, peace, kidney stone, or whatever. When I was having a kidney stone attack, no one would've looked at me and thought, he is being equanimous. I was rolling around the bed moaning like anyone else because it hurt. I was not saying, "Oh, there's a kidney stone, I'll smile like a Buddha?" Nonsense.

Know that you're free and be done. What's the benefit to this? When anger appears, it also disappears very naturally like the wave. But what we do is try to go into it to resolve it, change it, figure it out, or be equanimous with it. Then the wave just stays around for much longer because we're empowering it with validity, that it means something. "I got angry and I wasn't being equanimous. I am so unenlightened. I have to work at my equanimity and I am a loser."

You see, that wave doesn't get to pass by itself. That wave is completely natural; it comes, and it goes. Stop trying to be something other than who you are, now. If anger is appearing in that moment, that's what you are, anger. What is, is.

Liberation is very simple, three words: what is, is. That's all that needs to be said for liberation, what is, is, period. When that's fully reckoned with, what more is there? There's no self in here trying to manipulate or become something other than what is because you know what is can only be what is. There's no other choice, there's only now. Whatever is now, is truth. And anything that is not now, like, "I should be equanimous," or "I should be more enlightened," is not true, is it? When anger is appearing, that is true. Liberation means you stop arguing with what is.

Do you see the difference between this and equanimity? Equanimity means that there's a controller in there that has to be equanimous in the face of anger, so you're making two of yourself.

You don't need to be equanimous, you don't need to be anything. This is freedom, isn't it? Stop arguing with what is. That's the peace that passes understanding—not arguing with what is anymore.

> **Inquirer:** *On the path, I've noticed everyone is trying to not be angry, not be jealous, not be envious, etc. By thinking they fail every single time, it just grows and it blocks...*

Sal: That's right. You now see how you're operating. Why would people think, "I shouldn't be angry, and I shouldn't be jealous," or "I should be equanimous?" That's the data that's been programmed into this hard drive, by culture and religion. It's not original, you didn't come out of the womb saying: "Oh, I have to be equanimous." You learned that you shouldn't be angry, you shouldn't be jealous, and you should be equanimous. That's just data programmed into the brain's hard drive. You operate like this because culture programmed this ignorance into your head.

In truth, trying to be equanimous doesn't work because if anger is going to appear, it is going to appear. Tough. Anger doesn't care if you're trying to be equanimous or not. The anger usually wins. It's like you have a little person inside saying, "I have to be equanimous," and the anger says, "You lose and I win."

Most people on the path are still moralists, they speak about right behavior as if they had the inside scoop about what is right and wrong. "Don't get angry. Don't do this or that." They will judge you based on their beliefs. This has nothing to do with liberation.

Have a holiday and see that what is, is, and that no matter what is appearing now, you are aware, free.

> **Inquirer:** *This week has been a test. There's been a lot of yanking.*

Sal: I am glad to hear it because if nothing negative happens in the course of our work, then you will easily be fooled. For example, if you're in a meditation intensive for a month and you're in bliss the whole time, you think, "Oh, I am so enlightened." Then a month later you get hit over the head by some circumstance and you think, "Oh no, what happened to my enlightenment?" The real grace is not bliss; it is all the negative stuff that makes you recognize what's true, in the midst of it. In the midst of all of those complicated circumstances, enlightened or not, are you free? Have a holiday, now.

> **Inquirer:** *I've been yanked so much, and I just hear your voice say, "Have a holiday," and then, "Oh yeah," for a few seconds.*

Sal: That's all it is. You just recognize for a moment, "I am always free." There's no problem, even in the midst of trying circumstances, which are always going to be there. Life is not meant to be always easy and pleasant. You've seen for yourself that you've actually always been free, haven't you? You just didn't know it before. Is it true or not?

> **Inquirer:** *It's true.*

Sal: You also see that all experiences pass. So, don't be concerned. We have a shift and we come to know something different—I am free no matter what is appearing. So what if there's mental or emotional turmoil? It's natural. Of course, it's going to happen for anyone. We're not trying to get into a state where we are untouched by anything. Freedom is the natural human condition; you've seen that for yourself. We think on the path that we are going to attain some state where nothing ever touches us. That is simply not natural.

⟅⟆⟆

Tendencies

> *Inquirer: What we have been exploring is true. I get caught up in my habitual tendencies and old habit patterns. That's what needs to be weakened.*

Sal: Don't give them any power at all. There's nothing there.

> *Inquirer: I'm just saying, that's what distracts.*

Sal: Why wouldn't it? After a lifetime of those beliefs, why would your seeking tendencies be immediately gone once you recognize truth? That is not natural for anyone. It does take a bit of time.

However, have a look. Where are those tendencies and impressions, now? They don't exist. Don't believe in this subconscious nonsense. If you do, you are right back on the

Freudian psychological carousel. Get real, jump off the carousel. Where are they, now? I don't see them.

> **Inquirer:** *Right. We don't see them because we are attentive right now.*

Sal: We don't see them because they don't exist. There is only now. They're not lurking behind somewhere. There's only now, and now, they don't exist.

So fine, a doubt comes up tomorrow, no problem. It is natural. I say, one day it won't happen anymore; but it's not to have a goal or expectation of that because it is already finished, now. This is very important to hear. If this is reckoned with, now, it is already over.

Yes, it can take a bit of time for you to be doubtless, that's all. I just don't want to give these tendencies and impressions any power because that is once again, giving them belief and that is the on switch to delusion, isn't it?

> **Inquirer:** *Yes.*

Sal: If you believe tendencies are little rascals in there, then you believe they exist. Freedom is the end of belief. So, without having any expectations, it will be finished, but don't think about it like that. Just know, now, that you are free. There is only now. Now they are not here.

⎯ ⎯ ⎯ ⎯ ⎯ ⎯

Being Finished

Inquirer: I have a fear that it won't be completely finished. I just want it completely done. I guess that's the fear that I have. Meeting you and seeing this has been the most amazing thing, but I need to know, I need to see this all the way through.

Sal: Then it's a done deal. You cannot fail. I am telling you right now, hear these words, you can't fail, and you won't. There's nothing to gain anyway. Let's have a holiday, now.

You know what's true, don't you? Any doubt?

Inquirer: No.

Sal: Let me ask you this: right now, forget the future, isn't it already finished?

Inquirer: Yes, it's always been finished.

Sal: So, the only thing is that there are thoughts that appear like there's something more or there's something not finished. But those are just thoughts, aren't they?

> *Inquirer: Yes, I guess it's just a subtle belief in separation or self, with a history. It's so helpful to hear, "What do you want?" That just dissolves the story.*

Sal: Then, I have to say (not that you can do or not do this), don't have the desire that you want it to be finished sometime in the future. Just notice that it's already finished, now. You just said it is. So, it must be true.

> *Inquirer: Yes, I guess if I want that in the future, I will always want.*

Sal: Yes, but what is that wanting? That wanting is a tendency, an impression that there is something wrong. It's just a thought, isn't it? Why is it appearing? It's been appearing your whole life. Why wouldn't it appear a few more times?

> *Inquirer: Yes, and I get comforted by the fan analogy.*

Sal: Yes, it will appear until it doesn't appear anymore, that's all. It's just appearing once in a while because it's the momentum of your whole lifetime. It may appear a few more times. But it's nothing. It's ephemeral and it's just a thought, here and now, meaningless, absolutely meaningless. Just get real, don't buy it.

Don't believe that belief. There's nothing you can do or can't do about that. I just put another impression in your head that says, "Don't believe the belief." Now, that impression is there, "Don't believe the belief," and you won't. You're not doing that, but it will appear. You can see it's already attained, and always has been attained.

> **Inquirer:** *Yes, it has always been here. Just getting the clouds (doubts)...*

Sal: There are no clouds either, by the way. Don't look for clouds. Where are they? It's just a belief. A belief that there are clouds. The clouds, apparent clouds, are not separate from you either, just like the wave and the ocean. In that moment, when you're seeing a cloud, a doubt, you're seeing yourself appearing as a doubt.

You will be finished. It will be finished for you, don't worry.

It's already finished.

ALSO BY SALVADORE POE

The Way of Freedom

To find out more about Salvadore's other writings,
inquiries and events

visit:

www.liberationis.com

www.salvadorepoe.com

CPSIA information can be obtained
at www.ICGtesting.com
Printed in the USA
LVHW041430070219
606759LV00003B/665